Rights across Borders

Rights
across
Borders

Immigration and the
Decline of Citizenship

DAVID JACOBSON

The Johns Hopkins University Press
Baltimore and London

The Johns Hopkins University Press
2715 North Charles Street
Baltimore, Maryland 21218-4319
The Johns Hopkins Press Ltd., London

Library of Congress Cataloging-in-Publication Data will be found
at the end of this book.

A catalog record for this book is available from the British Library.

ISBN 0-8018-5150-5

To Sharon

Contents

Acknowledgments

Researching and writing this book has provided me the opportunity to talk to a variety of people across different disciplines and in different places. This book is, in one sense, a record of a journey, both literally and figuratively. It is my pleasure to note here my debt to some of my fellow travelers.

My colleague and friend George Thomas has been of great help and our many discussions, particularly on theories of the state, certainly pushed this project forward. I am deeply indebted to John Boli for his careful reading of the manuscript and for his invaluable comments. Richard Ashley brought his considerable intellect, as well as his pithy comments, to my aid at certain critical junctures. (Not least, I am grateful to him for helping me with the title of this book.) I am grateful to Emanuel Adler for the frequent discussions we had in the formative stages of this project. My thanks to Suzanne Keller, Yasemin Soysal, Roxanne Doty, Noah Pickus, Bernie Farber, Rose Weitz, John Meyer, Dan Jacobson, David Goldberg, Gilbert Rozman and Paul Starr for their comments and suggestions at different points of the study. The members of the ASU colloquium on Global and International Studies provided many helpful comments as well. I appreciate Richard Brown's extensive help in facilitating access to legal materials.

I am indebted to Esther Hardesty, Rick Sears, Sandi Balistreri, Steph Lambert, J. R. Woodward, Elizabeth Sims, and Nelta Edwards for research and administrative assistance.

Early research on immigration to the United States was supported by an award from the John D. and Catherine T. MacArthur Foundation, and the Center of International Studies at Princeton University. This study also benefited from a year I spent as a Visiting Fellow at the Leonard Davis Institute of International Relations at the Hebrew University of Jerusalem. A Faculty-Grant-in-Aid from Arizona State University provided essential research support.

Most of all my thanks and love go to my wonderful family, my wife, Sharon, a true *eshet ha'il*, and our beautiful children, Adam and Maya. Surely children are the blessing of this world. Among my greatest debts are those to my parents. My mother died more than twenty years ago; I only wish she were here today to see the book (and, even more, to see all her grandchildren). She would not have been surprised by the topic.

Rights across Borders

1

Novus Ordo Seclorum

The American and French revolutions, arguably the historical fountain-heads of the nation-state, not only "reinvented" government and society but promised to reshape the world order. The revolutionary declarations and statements of these new nations referred not only to republican rule and the rights of the citizen but also to a vision of a *novus ordo seclorum* in the world as a whole. These revolutions were foreign as well as domestic, and the aspiration for "self-government" had both international and societal implications.

The Declaration of Independence reveals an acute sensitivity to America's place in the world. The principles of equality and national self-determination were to apply to all nations. The United States sought "separate and equal station" among "the Powers of the Earth." Like all nations, the United States is accountable to these principles of universal significance. Thus, "a decent respect to the opinions of mankind" requires that the United States must explain the causes that "impel" it to separation. The government—the state—represented "the People," and "whenever any Form of government becomes destructive of these ends," the People may alter or abolish it. A nation-state was born. Similarly, the Declaration of the Rights of Man and Citizen, embodied as the preamble of the French constitution of 1791, asserted the equality of all men, the sovereignty of the people, and the inalienable rights of the individual as universal principles.

If governments are to represent the people, if the state is to be projected as the embodiment of the people, to be a nation-state, the people must be actively involved in their government, they must be citizens rather than mere subjects; the people must have rights to ensure government accountability. The founding documents of the United States and revolutionary France contain a panoply of such rights concerning freedom of speech, association, the vote, and so forth. However, it was understood that such rights, though of universal import, could only be realized in the national framework. Libertarian rhetoric is tied to a more centralized, national state. Freedom is expressed through the nation. Self-government is an expression not only of individuals freely choosing their representatives but also of the nation expressing its sovereignty. Democracy is historically rooted in the rise of nationalism.[1]

Human rights—beginning with the Universal Declaration of Human Rights, adopted by the United Nations in 1948 and the trunk from which other human rights codes grew—are drawn in inspiration and partly in content from the Declaration of Independence, the United States Constitution, and the Declaration of the Rights of Man and Citizen.[2] The Universal Declaration includes such rights as the right to opinion, to religious freedom, to association, and to own property. In contrast to the abstract references to cross-national "inalienable rights of Man" in the founding documents of nation-states, human rights are highly elaborated and formalized. More importantly, whereas civic (national) rights can only be realized by "a People," one does not have to be part of a territorially defined people or nation to enjoy human rights. Human rights are not predicated on nationality.[3] Human rights are not based on the distinction between "national" and "foreigner" or alien (although international law does not prohibit such a distinction—see chaps. 4 and 5). Political, civil, and social rights within the state, however, are based on such a distinction.

The irony is that international human rights codes, rooted as they are in the documents establishing nation-states, are becoming the vehicle that is transforming the nation-state system. In the Euro-Atlantic core of the world order, in North America and Western Europe, the basis of state legitimacy is shifting from principles of sovereignty and national self-determination to international human rights. Increasingly, territorially delimited nations are not the only carriers of "universal humanity." All residents, noncitizens as well as citizens, can claim their human rights. In this process the state is becoming less constituted by "the people" while becoming increasingly constituted by international human rights codes and institutions. The state is becoming less a sovereign agent and more an institutional forum of a larger international and constitutional order based on human rights. Individuals and nonstate entities are increasingly able to partake in shaping the international legal order through the forum of the state and are becoming international, indeed transnational, actors in their own right.

International human rights claims in the immediate postwar period were a function of states representing those with human rights claims, and thus did not challenge the sovereignty of the state. Since the 1970s, however, individuals and nonstate entities have increasingly been able to make claims on their own states, and cross-nationally on other states, on the basis of international human rights codes, or instruments.

When one considers that the origins of human rights inhere in the very birth of the nation-state, the intricacy of social change becomes apparent. Human rights evolve from the nation-state, a step, so to speak, in a historical progression. Yet human rights transcend, adapt, and transform the nation-state.[4] No form of social or political change is de novo, no matter how radical.[5] What we are witnessing today is the transforming of the state and international institutions, of their function and of their very *raison*, and human rights provide both the vehicle and object of this revolution.

Human rights codes are taking on such salience not because of any intrinsic normative concerns about human rights in the states involved. The rather marginal movements that devote themselves to human rights have not been a major factor either. International human rights have come to the fore as a result of the piecemeal and incremental strategies of states to confront growing transnational challenges.

In order to study this ongoing paradigmatic shift from state sovereignty to international human rights, this book considers the state's attempts to confront one such transnational challenge, transnational migration. It also examines the institutional reformations that are consequently taking place with respect to the state, international institutions, and nongovernment entities.

Defining a Nation

THE SOVEREIGN PEOPLE

With the American and French revolutions, and even perhaps as early as the Dutch Revolt and the establishment of the Dutch Republic in the seventeenth century, the idea that sovereignty resides with the people, rather than the monarch, began to take root.[6] Today, there is little question that "the people" are the source of the state's authority and sovereignty. This, after all, is what makes the state a nation-state—it is a state that, at least imputedly, represents or embodies the people. Sovereignty signifies the existence of a national community. Modern societies contain a multiplicity of associations, from churches and synagogues, political parties and voluntary associations, to businesses. The state is not the only agency. However, sovereignty is what distinguishes the state from other forms of association. "An ultimate unity of allegiance," wrote Harold Laski, is "a guarantee of order." The sovereign nation-state is the all-encompassing expression of the common bond that unites all on the basis of common citizenship. The state, within its domain, is universal in its grasp as it represents the one compulsory association.[7]

The broad acceptance of popular sovereignty, however, does not make the concept of sovereignty unproblematic. As Cynthia Weber notes, how the people are defined and who can speak for them are not axiomatic. The state has to ensure its "representativeness" in order to claim sovereign authority legitimately. The state politically represents the people through the elective and political process but that process is effective only through "symbolic" representation. The state is not only the "government"; it embodies the national myth, a sense of the national self, even a soteriological promise. If the state is unable to represent or symbolize "the people" in a credible way, then its authority, and its sovereignty, is in question.[8] This is, in great measure, the challenge to the legitimacy of the nation-state today in the United States and Western Europe; it is increasingly difficult for the state to maintain, control, and thus define the national and social boundaries of the body politic.[9]

This study focuses on transnational migration, such as illegal immigration and the use of "guest workers," since such a transnational challenge directly impinges upon the principle of citizenship and on how the nation-state draws its boundaries. Transnational migration brings into question the state's ability to define "the people." Transnational migration, furthermore, challenges the understanding that nationhood is necessary for the full realization of rights.

The sociological element in how the nation-state and state sovereignty are constituted is critical to understanding contemporary changes in domestic and international politics. Much of the discussion in international relations theory and in political sociology has tended to stress, implicitly or explicitly, the territorial dimensions of the state.[10] Although a distinguishing mark of the nation-state, a bounded territory is not so much *the* defining characteristic of the sovereign nation-state as a precondition for demarcating the boundaries of a national community.[11] A bounded territory is a way of determining who belongs to the national community and who does not, and who has access to it and who does not.[12] Hence the principle of nonintervention (that no state has the right to intervene in the affairs of another state), a principle designed to uphold and reinforce state sovereignty, does not concern territorial intervention as such. Rather, the "duty" of nonintervention applies, above all, to the relationship between a state and its citizenry, an area off limits to other states.[13]

The failure to appreciate fully the "peopleness" of the nation-state handicaps analysis of contemporary trends. As John Ruggie notes in another context, prevalent approaches that stress bounded territorialities in the study of international relations do not show "a hint that the institutional, juridical, and spatial complexes associated with the community may constitute nothing less than the emergence of the first truly postmodern international political form."[14] Consequently the impact of transnational migration and the regulation of immigration on the nation-state has been all but ignored by mainstream theorists of international relations and, until recently, viewed in narrowly demographic terms by sociologists.[15] Yet transnational migration concerns the "boundedness" of the nation-state and boundedness is at the very heart of the concepts of sovereignty and self-determination. The very process of self-determination concerns the drawing of boundaries, of borders, of stating that a nation is individual and unique. Making distinctions between citizen and alien is a crucial part of this process.

Membership, or determining who is a citizen, is a basic aspect of all other political and social issues in the nation-state because the criteria of membership determine the human fabric of the nation-state. Determining who may become a member and a citizen is the state's way of shaping and defining the national community. Immigration control—how and to what extent the state chooses to apply it—is consequently inherent in sovereignty. "Admission and exclusion are at the core of communal independence," writes Michael Walzer. "They suggest the deepest meaning of self-determination. Without them, there could not be *communities of character*, historically stable, ongoing associations of men and women with some special commitment to one another and some special sense of their common life."[16]

The ability of the state to patrol its boundaries, in a sociological as well as a political sense, is critical because if the state fails to do so, if "strangers" can enter a country at will, the ability of the state to shape and define a nation is compromised. In Cynthia Weber's words, the state must control how the people are "written" or constituted and how their meaning is fixed. If the state loses its claim to "representativeness," if it "loses its control to symbolize its people in believable ways, then it risks losing its source of sovereign authority."[17] In the age of popular sovereignty the state is rooted in the people and in representing the people, and when the state is unable to maintain a coherent sense of nationhood, the legitimacy of the state itself is in question. This is not only a question of statecraft however; there is a deeper sociological, even existential, meaning to controlling borders. "The social borders of a political community do not just have a functional meaning," Jürgen Habermas writes. "[T]hey regulate rather one's belonging to a distinct historical community linked by a common fate and a political life form that constitutes the identity of its citizens."[18]

Transnational migration is not the only transnational flow or activity that is posing problems for states' control of their boundaries and for state sovereignty. Indeed, transnational migration is associated with other transnational developments, such as the globalization of production, which are of great import for the emerging shape of global politics. Furthermore, developments such as global production in some respects create similar problems of representativeness for the state; this is evident in Robert Reich's question, "Who is us?" referring to the problem of determining which corporations serve the specifically national interest in a global economy.[19] Transnational political arrangements also pose questions for state sovereignty as do the transnational environmental challenges increasingly in the public eye. All these issues are related and all need to be (and are) separately studied. Yet the transnational flow of people draws our special attention as it is distinctly different from the flow of, say, oil. Transnational migration—the ability of the state to regulate it and its implications for nationhood in the host countries—has an immediacy for the "community of character" that other transnational flows simply do not.

Furthermore, insofar as the nation-state and its basis of legitimacy have been compromised in core regions of the world, the response to, and institutional developments in the wake of, transnational migration will give us an indication of emerging forms of political and social organization. In the final analysis, all political and social organizations are predicated on how "community" comes to be defined, be they medieval corporate groups, nation-states, or transnational ethnicities, to name a few.[20] Economic developments are central forces of change, but economic abstractions cannot be the basis of political and social association. The collapse of communism, the renewed nationalisms, and the difficulty of converting Eastern European economies to capitalism on the basis of Western academics' prescriptions are evidence enough of that. "How states respond to the increasing mobility of people," James Hollifield writes, "will tell us a great deal about the future of world politics and the prospects for a peaceful and liberal world order."[21]

International relations between the Euro-Atlantic community and the rest of the world are also implicated. As the idiom and claims of human rights reach across borders, so Third World countries reassert their sovereignty. These divergent discourses deepen the fissure between North and South. The emerging form of the state in the Euro-Atlantic core does *not* apply to the state in most of the Third World; nor does the Euro-Atlantic "model" suggest any *necessary* evolution of the state in other parts of the world.[22]

CITIZENSHIP

The French Revolution brought together the invention of the nation-state and the institution and ideology of citizenship. This was no accident, as citizenship and the nation-state are intricately linked to one another. Indeed, it is fair to say that citizenship is the linchpin of the nation-state. Citizenship fulfills two principle tasks: first, it determines the criteria of membership, that is, who may and may not belong to or join "the people"; and, second, rules of citizenship determine the nature of the "conversation" between the individual and the state—the rights and obligations of the citizen, the kind of access the citizen has to the state, and the kinds of demands the state can make upon the citizen.[23]

That conversation may concern the extent the state is responsible for the individual's welfare or the degree the right of privacy may be intruded upon in order to protect the general interest. Much of the debate about domestic politics in Western countries since the seventeenth century has been shaped by the guiding issue of where authority lies between state and society, concerning topics that range from pacifism to abortion. Thus citizenship has been construed in different ways, from the more interventionist approach in Scandinavia to the more classically liberal approach of the United States.

The focus here, however, is on the first aspect of citizenship—determining the criteria of membership in the nation-state. The two aspects are interlinked. As Habermas points out, the view that the expansion of domestic citizen rights is rooted in class struggle or, one may add, gender is too narrow an approach. Migration has been "a driving force" in expanding citizen rights.[24] Maxim Silverman notes how immigration has raised questions not only about membership but about rights.[25] More generally, the role of citizenship in defining the boundaries of the nation is linked to the domestic politics of citizenship. If the distinction between citizen and alien erodes, and the boundary defining the national community consequently is blurred, the civil connection between state and society becomes frayed. The state abdicates its role as the political organization of the community because there is less of a community to represent. In such circumstances, civic, economic and even political associations will decreasingly use the state's boundaries as a point of reference.

Customarily, laws of citizenship are presented in terms of *jus soli* (place of birth) or *jus sanguinis* (line of descent). In the Anglo-American tradition, principles of ascription and consent have competed for supremacy.[26] *Ascription* denotes that one's political membership is a function of an objective circumstance, such as birth within a particular jurisdiction. *Consent* suggests that political membership can emerge only from free individual decision. Observers have discerned basic differences in laws on immigration between nations that were constituted by immigration, such as the United States and Canada, and those that were not, such as the European countries. Nations that were constituted by immigrants have tended to be more inclusive.[27] The United States and Germany in this respect represent two polar cases, of an inclusive immigrant society and of an exclusive society based on national line of descent. The United States, following the Revolution, turned its back on the idea of a distinctive national (ethnic) or cultural identity, and chose to define itself in universal political terms. German nationality, in contrast, is particularistic and rooted in the bloodline of the *Volk*.

The Argument

Transnational migration is steadily eroding the traditional basis of nation-state membership, namely citizenship. As rights have come to be predicated on residency, not citizen status, the distinction between "citizen" and "alien" has eroded. The devaluation of citizenship has contributed to the increasing importance of international human rights codes, with its premise of universal "personhood." The growing ability of individuals and nongovernment organizations (NGOs) to make claims on the basis of international human rights instruments has implications well beyond the boundaries of the individual states such that the contours of the international, as well as the domestic, order are likely to change significantly.

Transnational migration is cross-border migration that has eluded state regulation. In the American case, illegal immigration, primarily from Mexico, has been the chief issue since the 1970s. In Western Europe, guest-workers from Turkey, Algeria, and Yugoslavia, among other countries, became by the 1970s permanent residents in Western Europe, despite the opposition of their host countries. The reasons for the failure of state control are different in each of the regions, but the effects are similar. Social, civil, economic, and even political rights have come to be predicated on residency, not citizenship (with some national variations). Citizenship, consequently, has been devalued in the host countries: aliens resident in the United States and in Western European countries have not felt any compelling need to naturalize even when it is possible.

The devaluation of citizenship, together with the weakening of sovereign control and the principle of national self-determination, creates questions about the legitimacy of these states. The ability of the state to govern comes into question, conflicts arise on immigration and foreign populations, and, most important, the "pact" between state and citizen is broken. That pact symbolizes the political-cultural integrity of the nation and also determines how politics should be conducted and how goods should be allocated.[28] What is the basis of state authority when such a pact is broken or strained? Who are "the people"? What is the relationship between the state, nongovernmental organizations, and international institutions and law?

As transnational migration breaks down the citizen-alien distinction, states turn in a piecemeal and incremental fashion to international human rights law (such as the U.N. human rights instruments or the European Convention on Human Rights). States must increasingly take account of persons *qua* persons as opposed to limiting state responsibilities to its own citizens. International human rights law, in contrast to national law, recognizes the individual as an object of rights regardless of national affiliations or associations with a territorially defined people. (It is important to point out that a simple causal relationship between transnational migration and international human rights is not being posited here. The international human rights instruments and institutions had to be in place. Other factors may have contributed to bringing human rights to the fore—for example, the "harmonization" of laws in Western Europe or the woman's movement. Nevertheless, transnational migration has a particularly significant role to play due to the stark affinity between the alien and the principle of personhood at the center of international human rights codes.)

Given the affinity between the status of resident alien groups and individuals and the stress of international human rights laws on "personhood," aliens turn to such international codes in making claims on the state. The aliens in question do not have to be migrants per se. Any aliens, even long-standing aliens, can exploit the changed social, political, and legal circumstances—such as a more prominent role for international human rights codes—to which transnational migration has contributed. And once these international codes take on such salience, they apply to all persons, whether they are aliens or not.

The concept of nationality is thus in the process of, in effect, being recast, from a principle that reinforces state sovereignty and self-determination (by giving the state the prerogative of defining its nationals) to a concept of nationality as a human right; the state is becoming accountable to all its *residents* on the basis of international human rights law. The individual, in place of the state, is becoming the object of international law and institutions. (Although the concept of *universal citizenship* could apply here, the term, for some readers, would wrongly imply the emergence of some kind of "global community.")

While the United States and Western European countries all do indeed turn to international human rights instruments in accounting for these transnational actors, some moved more quickly than others. The Americans are the most ambivalent in their move to international human rights instruments, and the French are somewhat slower than the Germans. This ambivalence is rooted in the more "elastic" political character of American and French national identities and institutions. Paradoxically, the ethnonationalistic basis of German nationhood and citizenship led the Germans to turn more readily to international human rights codes to account for the foreign elements in their midst; for the Germans, unlike the Americans or the French, concepts of nationhood left little room for "internally" accounting for the migrants.

The growing accountability of the state to international human rights codes and institutions, together with the fact that individuals and nonstate actors can make claims on those states in terms of international human rights codes, goes beyond the expansion of human rights *within* the framework of nation-states. These developments alter the character of the state in three respects. First, the basis of state legitimacy is in the process of shifting from an entity that embodies the people's will (national self-determination) to an entity that advances transnational human rights. The state is not exclusively constituted by "the people" so much as it increasingly justifies its actions on the basis of universal human rights. Second, the judiciary is playing a crucial role in this development. Third, the bureaucracy of the state shows signs of growing, paradoxically, as the state becomes the "caretaker" responsible for implementing international human rights.

What we witness, then, is not a zero-sum relationship between the state and the international institutional order where the state "concedes" authority to a supranational polity. International human rights instruments and institutions define specific tasks and a role for the state. The state itself is the critical mechanism in advancing human rights. Similarly, international human rights codes draw in wider swaths of the population—specifically foreign populations—into the legal web of the state. Although human rights claims can be made on the state, this wider scope also means that noncitizens have certain *duties* and obligations to the state, such as paying taxes or sending their children to state-sanctioned schools. Thus the process described here, involving the relationship between the state and international institutions and law, is a dialectical one: the state is becoming the mechanism essential for the institutionalization of international human rights. The state and the international order are, consequently, mutually reinforcing.

THE STATE OF THE STATE

Until at least the late 1980s, and in many respects even now, neorealist and structuralist theories of the state dominated in political science and in sociology. In these approaches the state is portrayed as the organization that has a "monopoly on the instruments of violence" in a fixed territory, and as the actual bureaucracy responsible for government. The states system is stressed in accounting for state "behavior" or development. Neorealists suggest that the international arena is anarchic; however, the formation of alliances by states seeking to ensure their preservation produces an international "structure."[29] Structuralists point to foreign and exogenous pressures on state development. Thus overwhelming international and military competition, coupled with crises within the state bureaucracy, help contribute to revolutions and political change.[30]

By suggesting that the bureaucracy of the state is, in effect, all there is to the "state" was a theoretically problematic perspective at the start; it is a particularly questionable approach now as such a limited focus is retarding analysis of the changing shape of the state and the states-system. A conceptual exclusion of questions about state legitimacy and its source of authority—that is, the *cultural* basis of the state—distorts the subtle yet fundamental changes taking place in international relations.[31] The world, as John Ruggie writes, "exists on a deeper and more extended temporal plane, and its remaking involves a shift not in the play of power politics but of the stage on which the play is performed."[32]

This is not to say significant contributions have not been made in attempting to come to terms with the state in both its bureaucratic and cultural dimensions. Cogent critiques were offered vis-à-vis neorealist and structuralist approaches. It was noted that the unusual commonality of state structures in the international order hardly suggests the absence of international norms. The very idea of a state is dependent on a wider system that legitimates the state's sovereignty and territorial jurisdiction.[33] Other criticisms attacked the structuralist propensity to focus on a "weak" or a "strong" state and to stress the autonomy and capacity of the state and the varying ability of a state to achieve its goals.[34] As George Thomas and John Meyer point out, we cannot determine what a strong state is, since many of the strongest polities in Western history have been associated with weak central bureaucracies.[35] They note that it is not clear whether the nineteenth-century American state was strong or weak. Conversely, the French and Prussian states had impressive bureaucracies, yet they had fragile relationships with their societies. Poststructuralists within international relations argue that international practices are embedded in implicit structures and challenge the neorealist assumption that the state is ontologically unproblematic.[36]

However, even these critics view, mutatis mutandis, the state as the organizing principle of international politics, at least at the present moment. International regime theory posits that international rules delineate codes of conduct for states in certain "issue areas," such as agriculture or trade and tariffs. Still, states constituted these regimes for their own benefit.[37] Structuationists still view the state as the "agent" in the international arena.[38] Poststructuralists, though they question the "stability" of the state and question the ontological presuppositions of the neorealists, still suggest that the state is (albeit regrettably) the center of exclusionary political activity.

The Stanford institutionalists in sociology have studied the uniform structures and policies of nation-states, and they deduce that world cultural structures produce this uniformity.[39] Studies of national constitutions also indicate a world polity and culture.[40] However, the institutionalist model still sees the world polity reinforcing the state as the authoritative actor of the world polity.[41]

THE JUDICIARY

The judiciary is at the forefront of contemporary political changes. The decisions of regional judicial bodies, such as the European Court of Human Rights and the European Court of Justice, as well as the growing importance of international human rights in national courts, are fomenting a "quiet revolution." Constitutional (judicial) politics is a fast growing phenomenon in even the parliamentary systems of Western Europe, adding to the role of the judiciary.[42] Increasingly, the judicial tail is wagging the legislative dog.[43]

The stress in the literature on the state as a bureaucracy and as a forum for power politics, within states and between states, has led many theorists to overlook the role of the judiciary. The impression is, apparently, that "real" politics takes place in the executive and legislative branches.[44] Once again, this conceptual blinder has limited analysis of the state and the system of states.

The critical role of the judiciary in social and political transformation is evident in the movement from feudalism to the early modern state. Royal courts were instrumental in relocating authority from the skein of local and decentralized feudal rights and privileges to the central monarchical governments.[45] From about the thirteenth century through as late as the seventeenth century, the monarchy's judicial apparatus, though only partially effective in establishing central jurisdiction, built up precedents and compromises—lords here willingly submitting, there resisting, here grudgingly complying. Over time an effective body of law emerged that did in fact undermine the authority of the feudal lords. The broader significance is that with the transfer of judicial jurisdiction and body of law went the transfer of authority and the construction of sovereignty at the political center.[46]

The new, centralized states promoted national loyalties in place of feudal commitments. In this regard the notion of the citizen was crucial in cementing the authority of the central state (and in making monarchies more representative, ultimately "nationalizing" them into nation-states).[47] The centralized state in turn aided the principle of individual rights. Citizen rights freed individuals from traditional authorities and weakened such local authorities vis-à-vis the state. Social movements arose as groups denied rights, such as women, certain economic classes, and religious and minority groups, pushed for inclusion. As more groups were included in the body politic in this dialectical fashion, the jurisdiction and authority of the state grew.[48]

From the perspective of this study, the critical point is that authority was transposed from local entities to more central polities with the aid of judicial systems that spanned "local" units and began, if at first only rhetorically, to gain greater prestige.

STATE BUREAUCRACY

The irony is that while the growing importance of international human rights codes is gradually "relocating" authority and legitimacy from the state itself to a transnational order based on human rights, the state as a bureaucratic apparatus may well grow (and already shows signs of doing just that). As a bureaucratic entity the state's reach has, historically, steadily increased as larger proportions of the population came to be included in the sovereign body politic and as rights were expanded socially and economically as well as civically and politically.[49]

The increasing salience of transnational human rights does not preclude continuing growth of the state *as a bureaucracy*. As a caretaker responsible for human rights, the state still can increase its bureaucratic responsibility over populations. For example, a state can justify expanding its authority over a "positive" right such as education by using human rights discourse to argue that it must guarantee an education for everyone within its borders; alternatively, individual demands on the state to fulfill human rights might have the result of increasing its bureaucratic reach. The growth of state bureaucracy is apparent both under the impact of transnational migration (see chap. 2 and 3) and under the aegis of international human rights institutions (see chaps. 4, 5, and, in particular, 6).

Despite such counterintuitive increases in the state's responsibilities, however, its source of authority, its basis of legitimacy, is increasingly being "externalized" to the international human rights order. Nation-states have always, as noted earlier, legitimated themselves on universal notions of rights but such rights were construed nationally; a territorially bounded people or nation had to be available or imputed to constitute the state. Now all persons, citizen or alien, are more able to assert "rights" on the basis of codes that are not anchored on citizenship status but are much more elaborated and formalized than ever before.

The expansion of the state bureaucracy does not mean that that the bureaucracy is expanding in all its facets and in all respects, nor does it mean this process will be smooth and linear. Thus, in the area of ensuring human rights the state bureaucracy has generally expanded. On the other hand, the presence of migrants and foreign populations has been associated with declining support for state welfare benefits. Thus, in Western Europe and in the United States, migrants and illegal immigrants have fed calls for cutting back "the welfare state."

In sum, the state in the Euro-Atlantic core is in the process of becoming an institutional mechanism of a transnational order based on human rights. The relationships between nongovernment entities, the state, and international institutions show signs of being rearranged. Individuals and NGOs can make claims on the state on the basis of international human rights—whether on the state in which they are domiciled or on other states. This means that debates about the international legal order are increasingly conducted by individuals and nonstate actors through the forum of the state. NGOs are thus becoming agents that reproduce and transform the international legal order. The state's jurisdictional and judicial role and the relationship of the state to the individual or the NGO is becoming rooted in the international human rights legal order.

In analyzing the increased salience of international human rights law in Western Europe and the United States, it must be acknowledged that this is not an irreversible process. Transnational migration has contributed to civil dissension and ethnic tension in Western Europe.[50] More violent subnational splintering along national and ethnic grounds is conceivable, even in Western Europe. However, given the fundamental changes that migration, for one, has already wrought on concepts of citizenship, significant reversals of recent developments are unlikely. Past clampdowns on foreign residents and past opposition of the kind evident today has not lessened in a significant and ongoing way the foreign presence in Western Europe or the population of illegal aliens living in the United States.

Plan of This Book

The history of transnational migration, the failure of state regulation, and the impact of migration on citizenship in Western Europe are studied in chapter 2. France and Germany are a special focus. Their different concepts of nationhood and citizenship and their respective approaches to the migrant populations are outlined. France and Germany are of particular interest as they have by far the largest non-European Union (EU) foreign populations (some 68 percent) as well as the largest intra-EU foreign population (58 percent) among EU countries. Furthermore, France and Germany have strikingly different concepts of nationhood. Their differences vis-à-vis transnational migratory challenges can thus be compared.

Chapter 3 discusses the evolution of American nationhood and concepts of citizenship in the context of immigration law. The American case is studied not only because of its importance in the world order in general and in the Euro-Atlantic core in particular but also because the United States has been host to the largest influx of illegal immigration of any Western country. Furthermore, American conceptions of nationhood are unique and provide us another contrast vis-à-vis the French and German cases. The chapter examines the history of illegal immigration, and the history of attempts to control the entry of illegal aliens, culminating in the Immigration and Reform Control Act of 1986. The reasons for the failure of the attempts to control illegal immigration and its implications for the value of citizenship are analyzed.

Chapters 4 and 5 look at the shift to international human rights codes in Western Europe and the United States. The state's response to this transnational challenge and shift to international human rights instruments is documented. This has been a piecemeal and incremental process. It must be stressed the states concerned were not seeking new institutional arrangements as such. The states were responding to transnational challenges with the institutional mechanisms available to them—the long-term implications were not anticipated. In the Western European case, the European Court of Human Rights is the principle object of study because of its centrality in shaping national responses and laws in the area of human rights. The linkages with, and implications for, the European Union are briefly considered. The case of the United States' is developed in the context of its ambivalent legal history vis-à-vis international human rights law, and its attempts to confront illegal alien populations through constitutional law. Here the hitherto limited use of international human rights law (compared with that of the Europeans) is likely to change.

Chapter 6 turns to the implications of the changes documented in the previous chapters for the relationship between international and regional institutions, for the state and nonstate entities and individuals, and for the shape and form of domestic and international politics in the Euro-Atlantic community. The special role of the Organization for Security and Cooperation in Europe (OSCE) is discussed.

The concluding chapter reflects on changing understandings of community and territoriality. We live in a world where the patchwork of neighborhoods increasingly reflects international, not domestic, affiliations. Even "nationals," classically understood, increasingly fear that they will become foreigners in their own countries as the cultural, ethnic, and religious hues of "their" homeland become ever more nuanced. Living in a "diaspora" is becoming a common experience. Conversely, domestic society has become a partial microcosm of the world-at-large: North-South divisions have been domesticated and are no longer a preserve of the international arena. This chapter discusses the deterritorialization of identity, the progressive and ongoing breakdown of the belief that political identity and, hence, political agency are functions of the sovereign control of a territory. It ends with a consideration of the risks and promise of such a development.

2

Immigration and Citizenship in Western Europe

Once upon a time, writes Joseph Strayer, a man without a family, a lord, a local community, and a church was socially of little worth. Sacrifices of life and property were made for that same family, lord, community, and religion. The state was generally remote and of little importance. Kingdoms in the Middle Ages were based on personal loyalties and not on loyalty to abstract concepts like the "nation" or to ideologies and impersonal institutions. Power, as a consequence, was difficult to exercise at a distance; local representatives of a king tended to become rulers of their own. Power was tested anew every time there was a demand for a service. Such kingdoms often lacked continuity in time or space. Some kingdoms rose and fell in a historical moment. Others shifted in fantastic ways; the kingdom of the West Goths moved from the Baltic to the Black Sea to the Bay of Biscay in a few generations.[1]

Medieval society was made up of civically inactive persons, of nonparticipants. Medieval political life was radically fragmented and decentralized. Social horizons usually did not extend beyond the family, manor, or shire; very rarely did politics extend to the level of public concern. Indeed, feudalism almost precluded political relations. Relations were based on family and private treaty, and were patriarchal and affective. Bonds of personal allegiance were hierarchically arranged. Kinship and fealty precluded civic association. Dynastic ambition ruled out programmatic ideologies. Medieval life, devoid of public vision or a self-conscious citizenry, consisted of subjects, who obeyed. In a hierarchical and deferential world, independent, civil politics were inconceivable.[2] Only in the Italian city republics were civil politics evident.

The "diplomacy" of medieval Europe reflected its feudal makeup. Diplomats were messengers for a myriad of private parties. Kings made treaties with vassals; vassals made treaties with vassals. Kings received ambassadors from their subjects, or from the subjects of other princes. Diplomacy was, in effect, simply a formal means of communication in a hierarchically organized society. It carried none of the trappings that signified sovereignty, such as resident embassies or diplomatic immunities. Ambassadors were termed "public officials," but the public to be served was a unified *Republica Christiania*. (Similarly, the prince was expected to enforce not only his own municipal law, but also the common law of the whole community.) The reception or sending of envoys was not considered to be a sign of sovereignty or respect. (In the Italian city republics, however, diplomacy became an expression of shifting political loyalties and the rise of civil politics. Significantly, in parts of Italy organized foreign offices and permanent diplomatic agents were established.)[3]

The curious aspect of feudal Europe, however, was that nearly all "political" communication was of a private diplomatic sort—a means of upholding the personal and contractual ties that bound the prince with his vassals. Thus central political institutions were akin to diplomatic meetings rather than to practices of representation and government. Similarly in diplomacy or war, a ruler might find that one of his men had switched loyalties to a rival. It was as if, Donald Hanson writes, a state governor in the United States chose to change loyalties from the president to, say, the leader of the Mexican government. An inconceivable notion in the nation-state was not uncommon in the Middle Ages.[4]

No wonder then the concept of migration was of little consequence in the medieval period. Personal ties defined rule, not territory, and the state, such as it was, was not a territorial entity (and could itself "migrate").[5] The abstraction of a "people" or an "imagined community" was inconceivable, let alone the distinction between citizen and alien implicit in nationhood.[6] Similarly, the distinction between "domestic" and "international" relations did not resonate in the feudal context.

From the seventeenth century, territorial rule under a centralized and, usually, absolutist government emerged as smaller territories were forcibly absorbed into larger ones. This led to a relatively small number of independent states in competition with one another. This competition encouraged the rulers to strengthen domestic political and economic control. The policy of mercantilism broke down local economic autonomy and brought about a national and relatively unified economy, which, it was thought, would contribute to the national strength in the struggle with other states.[7] Population, in this absolutist period, was considered an economic and military resource, and territorial boundaries were assiduously policed to confine that "asset."[8] Thus with the rise of centralized states arises the distinction between national and foreigner and, concomitantly, an interest in regulating the international movement of people.

Furthermore, and perhaps more critically, the Reformation placed a premium on identifying the loyalties of the populace and ensuring more homogeneous populations. Consequently, groups that carried the faith of opposing states were often expelled. The number of Protestants, Catholics, Jews, and Moriscos expelled reached one million between 1492 and 1713.[9] Religious affiliation proved to be the basis of a protonationalism, instilling an identification with embryonic French, Dutch, and English nationalities, among others. The policies of absolutist rulers, whatever their motivations, resulted in the creation of states with large populations, often with a common language, who shared a common identification and affiliation with the state.[10] The Peace of Westphalia of 1648, widely viewed as the institutional beginning of the states system, is remarkable in this respect. Not only was a system of states, most led by monarchs, established, but states with unified and coherent populations (in the national sense) were promoted. The settlement of the Thirty Years' War ended the Holy Roman Empire as an effective institution and provided the legal basis for the states system. There was a virtual recognition of the independent status of the parties at Westphalia. The Dutch Republic and the Swiss Confederation were formally admitted to the family of nations. The Peace of Westphalia, the first multilateral agreement among independent states, marked the beginning of the balance-of-power system.[11] Most striking, however, was the enunciated principle of international relations following Westphalia—*cuius regio, eius religio* ("to each region, its own religion")—which anticipated the principles of sovereignty and national self-determination.

Mercantilistic control of the population eased by the middle of the nineteenth century. In the wake of the industrial revolution and its dramatic population growth, massive immigration took place, unfettered by state regulation. In the nineteenth and early twentieth centuries between sixty and seventy million Europeans left for better economic or political climes, primarily to the United States.[12] Migration between

European countries, however, was very modest. Before 1914, passports were not required in Europe outside of Russia. While the political and cultural roots defining a "national" can be traced back to the Reformation period, citizenship as such was not always central. In most countries, foreign populations were small, holders of foreign citizenship were barely recognized as aliens, and they were largely unaware that their legal status differed from nationals.[13] Nevertheless, foreign citizens could be deported if it was deemed that they were a political threat, criminally involved, or destitute or if deportation was otherwise deemed in the public interest.[14] By World War I states became much more centralized as a result of industrial growth; nationalism became more expressive in the face of international conflict. As laws on citizenship were tabled and strict immigration control followed, the nation-state reached full fruition. Nationality, carefully defined and protected, was now the basis for regulating relations among sovereign states.

With the growing stress on the state as a "representative" institution, an institution that embodies a people, boundaries needed to be drawn. How the national "self" (as in national self-determination) was to be constituted and, consequently, who the "other" was to be had to be elucidated. In the citizenship laws that were enacted around the turn of the century, those boundaries are sketched out, drawing on a variety of sociological, structural, and historical markers of nationhood. Here, from the Western European context, the French and German cases are highlighted.

Volkgeist and *Fraternité:* Nationhood in Germany and France

Of the European countries, France and Germany are of particular interest with respect to immigration, citizenship, and nationhood. First, they have by far the greatest number of non-European Union (EU) foreigners of any European country. In 1987 about 68 percent of foreigners in the then European Community (EC) and about 58 percent of intra-EC foreigners lived in these two countries. (The total foreign population was 13 million in 1987.)[15] Second, the two countries demonstrate, as a number of historians and sociologists have observed, remarkable contrasts in their concepts of nationhood.[16]

France and Germany represent, respectively, what Anthony D. Smith has referred to as a "territorial nation" and an "ethnic nation." In the first case, the nation is demarcated by the territorial and institutional boundary of the state. The sense of boundedness is critical for demarcating the national community. Such a nation is a nation of laws and legal institutions. The laws are derived from the state, and their uniformity and standardization reflect the sovereignty of the state. The "legal concept of the nation" also pointed the way for attaining nationhood through a model of "state to nation," a model emulated, with varying degrees of success, by many Third World countries in the period of decolonization.[17]

In the second case, the nation is organized politically on the basis of preexisting ethnic ties through a process of "mobilization" and "territorialization." The "nation to state" model stresses more "folkish" concepts of the nation and a common blood descent is emphasized. Customary and linguistic ties define the cultural markers of nationhood. Legal codes, though they of course exist, are not the basis for bonding the nation.[18]

France is the archetypical example of a nation that was shaped by the territorial and institutional frame of the state. French nationhood, writes Rogers Brubaker, was politically constituted, yet it is expressed in the striving for cultural unity. The French state developed over centuries and served as the point of reference in defining the parameters of the French nation. The territorial and institutional dimensions of nationhood led to an assimilationist approach to regional and cultural minorities. Citizenship is defined in broad terms such that today second-generation immigrants are automatically transformed into fellow citizens.[19]

The French state is an assertively unitary state and there is a sharp bifurcation between what is "French" and what is "foreign." Thus while both France and the United States welcome outsiders into the body politic, France demands complete assimilation into French culture and identity. American-style hyphenated identities are largely excluded in France. As Donald Horowitz puts it, France worships at the shrine of the common citizen, whereas the United States worships at the shrine of constitutional rights and ethnic pluralism.[20]

The French Revolution was decisive in inventing a nation and in creating a seemingly irrevocable link between the state and the nation. Central to the Revolution was the belief that all nations are the object of the same laws. The revolt against the monarchy was the first step in bringing liberty not only to France but to all nations, part of a general movement and a universal morality that would spread to all parts of Europe. "It is pretty certain," wrote the French minister of foreign affairs, Pierre Lebrun, in 1792, "that our principles will spread everywhere by themselves . . . precisely because they are principles of pure reason."[21]

This was a cosmopolitan revolution, with the nation defined through the state and the law. This was not a case of a nation in search of a state but a state (and intellectuals) in search of a nation (which, in turn, would legitimate state power). The "people" had to, in effect, be invented. The French statesman and a drafter of the Declaration of the Rights of Man and Citizen, Emmanuel Joseph Sièyes, expressed the prevailing opinion that the third estate was the nation. The nation, in turn, was an orderly association of individuals living under a common law. "The people were sovereign," Hans Kohn writes, "but they derived their power from the law, and the law derived its power from reason." With the nation's boundaries set in legal codes and institutions, membership had an ideological, rather than an ethnic, quality. Republicans of the time, such as Washington and Madison, were bestowed French citizenship.[22] The constitution of 1793 granted voting rights to foreign citizens living in France.[23] Conversely Tallien remarked in 1795 that the "only strangers in France are the bad citizens."[24]

Yet rational and universal "cosmopolitanism" had a Janus-faced quality; it also led to imperious and imperialistic endeavors. The French Revolution's message of liberty, fraternity, and equality was spread by France's armies to the rest of Europe in the guise of France as the most rational, enlightened, and advanced civilization. German nationalism, and the idea of an organic nation, a *Volk*, arose in the context of the Napoleonic wars. Liberty here took on the connotation not of a people freely determining a form of government and of a state rooted in popular consent. Here liberty looked outward: the "enemy" was not an anachronistic monarchy but an occupying French army, and liberty was freedom from foreign rule. Thus intimations of the *Volk* preceded the establishment of a German (nation) state by five decades. The conflict between France and Germany that would not end until 1945 was not simply a contest of realpolitik but of two visions of nationhood. Germany represented a nation in search of a state and, more than that, a protest against the rationalist and cosmopolitan beliefs of the French Revolution. Furthermore, the bourgeoisie who epitomized the Age of the Enlightment was much weaker in Germany than in the West.[25]

In contrast to French rationality and universalism, German nationalism developed a *volkisch* and particularistic character. German nationhood, nurtured by visionaries and intellectuals like Fichte, Hegel, and Schlegal, was rooted in the concept of the people as an organic cultural and racial entity marked by a common language. German nationalism, having preceded the political organization of the nation-state, was not identified with the state, or with the idea of citizenship. German national consciousness evolved from a preexisting cultural heritage.[26] The state, then, is the political representation of the *Volk*. For the French, conversely, the nation is identified with, and is a projection of, the state. Political unity and beliefs constitute the nation, not an ethnoculture. Nationhood for the French was thus inclusive and assimilationist, universalist and nationalist, and centered in the state.[27]

Two movements forged German nationalism—the romantic movement and the Prussian reform movement. For German romanticism, nations are unique, historical narratives of a particular spirit, a *Volkgeist* that is expressed in its culture, customs, law, and the state. The *Volk* is caught up in a historical progression toward freedom, an unselfconscious expression of its own uniqueness. An antistructural subjectivity was promoted against unfeeling rationality, "objectivism," and cosmopolitanism. The state becomes an expression of the *Volkgeist*.[28]

The Prussian reformers, on the other hand, wanted to duplicate the successes of France's postrevolutionary military. They sought to regenerate the Prussian state through deliberate state building, to mobilize the people around a *Staatsvolk*. This was a rational and conscious effort of administrators to create a powerful state along legal-rational lines.[29] In German nationalism, as a result, we witness a tension between *volkish* and political conceptions of nationhood. This creates problems of competing nationalist ideas. France never faced this problem as political and cultural elements were closely integrated and ethnocultural nationalism did not become deeply rooted.[30]

German unification in 1871 under Bismarck's guidance was motivated by military strategic concerns rather than *volkisch* nationalism. Nevertheless, the Reich was experienced as a nation-state. It largely succeeded in fusing the traditions of Prussian statism and *volkisch* nationalism. France suffered a succession of unstable regimes. But from 1830 the French nation state was consolidated. Both left and right shared a sense of France's mission in the world and of its national grandeur. French nationhood continued to be defined in essentially political, as opposed to ethnic, terms.[31]

The laws on attribution of citizenship were enacted in 1889 in France and in 1913 in Germany. These rules on attribution, with some modifications, remain in place today. Under the French law, citizenship was granted to all persons of foreign-born parents who were born and domiciled in France. Thus, as in countries of immigration, second-generation immigrants automatically become citizens. German citizenship law, conversely, does not recognize birth on German soil as a basis for citizenship. Citizenship is based solely on descent, following the principle of *jus sanguinis* rather than *jus soli*. In other words, the blood of the *Volk*, not ties to the soil, determined membership in the German nation. In most continental states, the principle of descent was complemented by the principle of birthplace and extended residence. In Germany citizenship is predicated exclusively on descent. Naturalization is only possible under very strict criteria.[32]

One finds a striking correlation between immigration and naturalization policy and the political cultures of the two countries. In line with the particularistic *volkisch* nationalism, Germany has never been an immigrant-welcoming country. The nine million ethnic Germans who migrated after World War II from Poland and other formerly German-occupied areas to West Germany were not, as Germans, viewed as "immigrants." Immigration law in Germany is better rendered as "foreigners' law" (*Ausländergesetz*).[33] France, on the other hand, long had a policy of attracting "assimilable" foreigners, primarily those from Catholic countries.[34]

The foreign workers who streamed into Germany and France, as well as other Western countries, entered on a legal and supposedly temporary basis. Once the presence of foreign workers became more permanent, however, the critical question was not so much immigration policy but the rules governing access to citizenship. Here, too, we find a strong connection between the political cultures of the two countries and their treatment of foreigners.

A host of data reflects the more open policies of France and the less welcoming policies of Germany. In 1980, 3.4 percent of foreigners in France acquired citizenship, through naturalization or attribution, whereas only 0.3 percent did so in Germany (excluding the acquisition of citizenship of persons from former German territories).[35] Average annual naturalizations in France from 1981 to 1989 were 8.5 persons per 1,000 residents whereas in Germany the comparable figure (from 1981 to 1988) is 1.5.[36] Nearly 13 percent of foreigners in France were naturalized between 1975 and 1984 compared with 6 percent in Germany.[37]

It takes eight years before aliens can apply for protected permanent residency status in Germany; even then, the decision is based on the degree of the applicant's acculturation. Foreigners in France wait for a much briefer period. Aliens in Germany have to wait ten years before applying for citizenship, whereas in France the wait is only five years.[38]

More significant than the voluntary acquisition of citizenship by naturalization, Rogers Brubaker observes, is the attribution of citizenship by the state in ways that are independent of the will of the person involved. France bestows citizenship on most persons with foreign parents born in French territory at birth or majority. Germany grants citizenship, as already noted, on the basis of descent; birth and prolonged residence have no significance in the attribution of citizenship.[39]

Patterns of social incorporation of alien residents also reflect models of nationhood. In France, the state plays a central and unmediated role in incorporating migrants in terms of their general welfare. Social functions are highly centralized around the state. In Germany, corporate groups, such as trade unions and social service organizations, are responsible for the welfare of migrants. These groups, however, are themselves centralized and have strong ties to the state.[40]

The impact of the differing policies on citizenship is, of course, that many immigrants have, or have the option to attain, citizenship in France, whereas only a small proportion of aliens in Germany can attain citizenship. (Across Europe, non-EU aliens have shown limited enthusiasm about obtaining citizenship, even when it is available.)[41]

Paradoxically, Germany adopted international human rights codes and the right of individual petition more readily than France. Germany finds itself with an increasingly large "foreign body," which it does not wish to absorb, nor can it expel. Germany, its domestic and international legitimacy in question, is thus more amenable to turning to international legal codes that take account of this anomalous situation. France, on the other hand, with its political definition of nationhood and its assimilationist tradition, has tried to deal with the migration problem domestically. France's response parallels to some extent the U.S. response to illegal migration (see chap. 3). France recognized the right of individual petition, including petition by aliens, under the European Convention on Human Rights (ECHR) only in 1981. Germany recognized such a right in 1955 and, more important, has renewed it ever since. France has incorporated the ECHR into domestic law in a legally ambiguous way. In Germany, the convention has been forthrightly incorporated into domestic law, and thus forms part of German federal law.[42] Even in France, however, the ability to deal with the migrant problem domestically has proved to be limited.

Europe: Guest Workers to Settlers

In regulating the flow of migrants (or any other cross-border flow), there are three possible points of interdiction: at the border, domestically, or in the country of departure. Domestic intervention in the area of immigration involves, inter alia, periodic document checks on local populations and employer sanctions. Intervention in the country of departure, which has generally remained a theoretical possibility, is usually framed in terms of foreign aid; financial and employment incentives are created to induce the migrant to remain in his or her home country.[43]

The problem of regulating transnational migration has been and is different in Europe than in the United States, and presents a different set of analytical problems. The American failure to stop physically or to impede substantially illegal entries has occurred primarily at the border. Subsequently attempts have been made to control illegal immigration through domestic measures. But the initial and critical failure was at the border. In the European cases migrant workers entered legally but supposedly for a limited time. Regulation has failed insofar as the European countries concerned were eventually unable to induce the large mass of "guest workers" to return to their home countries. The regulatory failure, in other words, was a domestic one.[44]

Thus, on the one hand, countries like Germany, where groups such as trade unions and corporations have strong ties with the state, could have more easily controlled illegal immigration.[45] Looser state-society ties create greater possibilities for transnational links, which in turn create domestic interest groups for the migrants vis-à-vis the state, as has occurred in the American case. Tighter state-society links generally imply greater coordination between the state and corporate bodies, which limits (but does not completely exclude) possibilities for transnational links of an illegal character. The decision to import guest workers was generally shared by the state, employers, and trade unions.[46]

On the other hand, the guest workers legally resident in the host countries could openly develop social and political ties and create associations to advance their interests. Over time, guest workers filled economic niches that local workers showed little interest in filling. Illegal aliens in the United States, in contrast, had to remain in the shadows, largely unorganized, fearful of deportation.[47] Guest workers openly developed a web of relationships with the host society. In fact, guest workers became an integral part of the host societies. As a consequence mass "rotation" back to their home countries became impossible by the 1970s and the Europeans realized that the guest workers had become settlers.

HISTORY OF THE GUEST WORKERS

Three phases can be identified in the migratory process to Western Europe: the migration of workers, which took place primarily from 1945 to the mid-1970s; family reunification in the host country, which began in the mid-1970s; and the transformation of migrants into permanent settlers, as ethnic minority communities formed.[48]

Mass migration and recruitment of foreign workers began in the immediate postwar period, increased in the 1950s, jumped dramatically in the 1960s and then almost stopped in 1973–74, when recruitment was halted. Most of the foreign workers came from Mediterranean countries, such as Turkey, Greece, Italy, Yugoslavia, Morocco, and Algeria. In contrast to the other European countries, Germany did not start recruiting foreign labor until 1956, as refugees from East Germany and the territories lost to Poland and the Soviet Union had filled the labor market up until that time. Britain, in most cases, ended migrant entries in 1962. The migrants were viewed as a strictly temporary necessity for the purposes of postwar construction. Migrants would return to their home countries once their economic role had been completed.[49]

In the first phase, the temporary status of the guest workers was supposedly ensured through the restricted duration of labor and residence permits. Foreign workers were often restricted to certain occupations and employers. Civil and political rights were limited. Labor permits, typically, could be revoked if the employment situation so required. Migrant workers themselves, by and large, had every intention of returning to their home countries after a few years. They sought to save enough to build a house or establish a business in their country of origin.[50] Thus for all parties concerned a "myth of return" was evident. Migration, it appeared, was controllable and reversible.[51]

The migration of workers reached a peak in 1970 and was followed by the immigration of family members, although available data do not indicate the precise time lag. After the halt of non-European Economic Community (EEC) migration in 1974 in France, family reunification accelerated, such that it became by 1980 70 percent of the total migration. In Germany the migration of women increased by over 6 percent and by 46 percent for children under sixteen years of age from 1974 to 1980. However, for men there was a drop of 5 percent for the same period.

Despite different immigration policies on family reunification between France and Germany, the results were similar. France, considering itself an immigration country, encouraged family reunification until some restraints were introduced in 1973. Germany stated that its labor recruitment excluded the immigration of family members. The policies affected the time lag between the phases of migration, but not the process itself. Even Germany could not halt the immigration of migrant family members or their entry into the labor pool.[52] With family reunification, permanent housing is sought, children go to schools, social services are called for—the settlement becomes permanent.

Mark Miller writes that postwar foreign worker policies were generated in a largely ad hoc fashion. Official assumptions about migration persisted even after they were shown to be misinformed. Some policies were not enforced and de facto new policies emerged.[53]

In France, the Office Nationale d'Immigration (ONI) was set up to organize foreign worker recruitment. French employers had to recruit through ONI. ONI statistics show that about 2 million European migrants and 690,000 dependents went to France from 1946 to 1970. Illegal entries as a proportion of all migrants increased from 26 percent in 1948 to 82 percent of migrants in 1968. It appears that the growth in foreign populations provided encouragement and support for clandestine immigration.[54]

In the early years, workers were mostly recruited from Italy, then later from Spain, Portugal, Yugoslavia, and Turkey. Until the late 1960s citizens of France's colonies and former colonies could freely enter France. By 1970 there were 600,000 Algerians, 140,000 Moroccans, and 90,000 Tunisians in the country. Overall that year there were 3 million migrants in France, 6 percent of the total population. Migrant workers were clustered in unskilled and semiskilled work in building, manufacturing, and services. Not until the guest workers began to bring their families to join them in France did the French government attempt to control immigration. At this time, however, their attempts were to little avail.[55]

Attempts were made in the early and mid-1970s to reduce the foreign worker population in France. Deportations of workers without documents were opposed with strikes. Financial incentives offered in 1977 for migrants who were prepared to leave were largely unsuccessful in inducing significant "rotation" back to their home countries. All these efforts had limited effect: the number of foreign workers fell from 1.8 million in 1973 to 1.4 million in 1981. However, the foreign population as a whole rose from 3.2 million in 1969 to 4.2 million in 1975, at which level it stabilized. Clearly, this reflected the process of family reunification. Those workers who left were more than made up for by migrant family entries and births in France. Furthermore, about 1 million people of migrant origin had been naturalized under France's relatively generous naturalization laws, making for a total of over 5 million with migrant roots.[56]

Like France, Germany set up a central recruitment office, the Federal Labor Office, through which companies could hire workers. Recruitment agreements were reached first with Italy, then later with Greece, Turkey, Morocco, Portugal, Tunisia, and Yugoslavia. Foreign workers numbered 95,000 in 1956 and reached 1.3 million by 1966. After a dip in foreign employment due to recession, the number of foreign workers reached 2 million by 1970 and 2.6 million by 1973. In the early 1970s workers began to bring their families to join them in Germany.[57]

In 1973, as social and political problems associated with the migrants grew, the German government halted further recruitment. Germany's suspension of immigration was more categorical than France's. Germany had made no commitment to settle the foreign workers, so it saw no inconsistency in ending recruitment or in repatriating unemployed foreigners. Furthermore, Germany refused work permits for spouses and children of foreign workers. Arrangements were made with Greece and Turkey for special German funds to aid migrants who returned.[58]

Foreign employment did decline from 2.6 million in 1973 to 1.9 million in 1976. Workers left because of withdrawn work permits or unemployment. But after 1977, foreign employment increased again as spouses and children filtered into the labor market. As Stephen Castles notes, when the need arose, some foreign workers were encouraged by employers to stay on, and those workers brought over their families. Large numbers of German-born children of migrants added to the foreign population. By 1981, the foreign worker population was around 2 million. The foreign population reached 4.7 million by 1982.[59] To these figures must be added the considerable numbers of refugees who have gone to Germany since this period and in particular since the reunification of Germany and the collapse of the Soviet Union.

Finally, the proportion of foreign populations in both France and Germany is also increased by the higher immigrant birthrates compared with the rates of the indigenous population.[60]

THE DYNAMICS DRIVING MIGRATION IN WESTERN EUROPE

Every corner of the globe has been drawn into the market economy. Subsistence economies have been uprooted, and growing numbers, as a consequence, are searching for work. Most will relocate within their own country, but many will try to move from the poorer South to the more promising North. The migratory movement is compounded by the much greater rate of population growth in the South.[61]

International migration, however, is not driven by the dynamics of international trade, economic models notwithstanding. When a country has a deficit in its balance of payments, indicating excessive imports, the value of its currency is reduced. Import costs increase, exports go up, and a new equilibrium is reached. No imbalance exists, as Myron Weiner notes, between emigration and immigration that needs to be corrected. The market does not correct itself by pushing up the economic costs of immigration. Economically speaking, there is no "excessive" immigration. But there are costs—in political, social, and cultural currency.[62]

Labor shortages in and of themselves do not necessitate the admission of migrants; wages can be allowed to rise, women and other populations that were outside the market can join the labor force, and there may be a shift from labor- to capital-intensive investments. In the 1950s and 1960s Japan's labor shortages matched those of Western Europe, but the Japanese, seeking to be ethnically homogeneous, rejected the option of importing Korean migrants as they had done in the 1930s.[63] Labor-intensive industries from Japan moved instead to Korea. The relatively small Korean minority that is in Japan is denied full membership rights.[64] (In the late 1980s and early 1990s, however, both legal and illegal entry of foreigners into Japan did increase substantially—a development that could have long-term consequences for Japan's otherwise successful containment of immigration.)[65]

Thus it is not sufficient to explain migration only in terms of contending, or "push-pull," economic forces. One needs to delineate under what historical conditions the economic factors came into play.[66] While in the United States a porous border facilitated massive illegal migration, this was not the case in Western Europe. Europe's borders were not overwhelmed. In the United States, employers hiring illegal aliens could, in effect, act independently of the government. In Western Europe a conscious decision was made, involving the state, employers, and even the unions, to import migrant workers. What were the considerations?

The extensive welfare benefits of Western European countries, specifically the benefits available for indigenous workers, provided the impetus for importing migrant workers. The welfare state is a closed system, Gary Freeman writes, because a national community requires a moral basis, a "community of character," in order to undertake mutual aid. But membership of such a community implies the exclusion of nonmembers from that process of sharing.[67]

Workers in welfare states receive compensation in two parts; the direct wage from the employer and the benefits, insurance, and guarantees they receive from the state—the indirect wage. The availability of benefits, the indirect wage, was critical in the decisions to import workers. Workers were not imported due to labor shortages per se. This was a political decision. Indigenous workers opposed movement to capital-intensive industry or avoided certain kinds of work altogether. Welfare support such as unemployment compensation facilitated such a position. Thus, employers looked to foreign labor. Temporary labor, lacking the indirect wage, is not only cheaper but is in theory more flexible. Temporary labor cannot fall back on welfare benefits to resist employer demands. Indigenous workers, unwilling to fill certain low-wage, unpleasant, and low-status jobs or give up their indirect wage, tacitly or even explicitly accept the importation of foreign workers. The state profits from temporary workers, as this frees the state from the burden of paying for unemployment support and other benefits. Hence, agreement was reached between the state bureaucracy, employers, and labor in the importation of foreign workers.[68]

In a functioning guest-worker system, unemployment benefits are not a problem. Migrants who become unemployed lose their work permits and have to leave. Temporary migrants are usually single, young, and healthy and make few medical demands. The single largest cost for the state is pensions for which few temporary migrants apply. In addition, the migrant workers come from countries where the life expectancy is much lower than in Europe. So even if the migrant workers were to request their pensions, they would not get them for as long. In other words, the migrant workers pay more in taxes and deductions than they will ever receive in services. That is if the guest system functions as it was meant to. But if the guest workers do not go home, then the picture becomes more cloudy. Family unification creates a new set of demands on welfare benefits, schools, and housing subsidies. The migrant workers themselves are drawn, over time, into the net of welfare benefits.[69]

Welfare benefits and citizenship status cease to be correlated. Entitlements to pensions, medical benefits, and unemployment insurance are often linked to deductions from wages. In this way, nonmembers (migrants) can benefit over the long term from welfare systems. Thus, the *settlement* of labor is a threat to the welfare state as it fragments the beneficiaries into members and nonmembers, which strains the moral glue of mutual aid.[70]

Thus, the state benefits, so long as the guest-worker system is truly temporary. The regulatory process, however, has proved to be flawed.

"THE WEB OF TIES": WHY THE REGULATORY PROCESS BROKE DOWN

The legal entry of the foreign workers allowed them openly to form associations and to establish ties with indigenous trade unions, political parties, and civic, church, and human rights organizations. In addition, bilateral treaties sanctioned the emplacement of migrant-support organizations that were affiliated with the home governments in the host countries. These associations and ties proved to be formidable forces in advancing migrant interests and in halting host governments attempts to erode the migrant presence, for example, in the area of family reunification.

The ties that the foreign workers established with political, economic, and civic organizations led to a conflict between the "private" interests of those organizations and the national interests of the state. Thus, the institutional distinction between state and society (which is so central to the definition of nation-states and liberal democracies) paradoxically provides structural opportunities for transnational relations. Private links of indigenous organizations with migrants (or other transnational groups) lead to local interests pressuring national governments in terms of those transnational concerns. Discrete and segmented foreign groups, history has shown, can be expelled relatively easily.[71] Once a "web of ties" has formed, however, such foreigners become a part of that society, be it German, French, or Swiss. Expulsion at that point becomes antithetical to those countries' democratic norms. But it is important to stress the interwoven character of structural factors (the associational ties that develop) and the normative dimensions.

In the early years of the foreign worker presence, certain groups, such as radical leftists and churches, rallied to the support of the migrants.

However, the foreign workers found themselves generally shut out of the unions and all political channels blocked. The migrants consequently resorted to extraparliamentary measures to protest work and housing conditions and racism. They undertook work stoppages, rent strikes, hunger protests, occupied houses and factories, and fomented riots. Such activities were the voice, as Mark Miller describes it, of the "institution-ally voiceless."[72] Thus migrants, though they do not have the traditional means to act upon the channels of authority or any "industrial rights" in the host countries, still have the opportunity to influence their working conditions.[73]

Foreign worker strikes, which often had anti-trade union tones, em-barrassed the unions and forced them to become more responsive to the migrants. Unions had to incorporate these workers in order to offset the risk that the migrants would establish autonomous and competing unions. Furthermore, union bargaining power, it was recognized, is tied to the degree of unionization. It is in the identification of "migrants" with "workers" that trade unions became an early "welfare agency" that protected their economic and social rights.[74] Although independent for-eign worker strikes continued at least into the 1970s, the strikes became less anti-union as the unions began to represent the foreign workers. Similarly, the migrants increasingly expressed their grievances through the mainstream labor movement. Representation of migrants in the unions in turn blunted the regulatory impact of the state. Thus, for example, when in 1975 France announced plans for suspending family reunification and stricter control over amnesty programs for illegal work-ers, migrant protests were supported by major trade unions, among other French organizations. As early as 1963, threats in Germany to deport foreign worker strike leaders in the steel industry were undermined because the strike was organized and supported by the I.G. Metall union.[75]

The foreign workers' work-related strikes had political offshoots. Industrial action became a step toward political participation. Migrant political movements formed in France. German unions backed greater foreign worker participation in local government. In both France and Germany, as well as other countries, the foreign worker protests pro-duced a twofold response by the national governments. The protests contributed to the governments' determination to end further introduc-tion of foreign workers and to institute stricter controls on illegal mi-grants in the mid-1970s. The recession following the oil crisis was also a contributing factor at this time. On the other hand, the governments reinforced or created institutional channels for foreign workers to represent their interests.[76] The web between the foreign workers and their host societies was spun ever tighter. Border controls were intensified, but internally the "foreigners" became integral elements of the countries concerned, and domestic regulation became ever more problematic.[77]

In addition to the unions, and prior to the mid-1970s when their status as permanent residents was recognized, the foreign workers could use a number of channels to put forward their concerns. Local consultative systems have been widely used since the 1960s. In Germany, where they were most developed, migrant parliaments, advisory councils, and migrant committees of local parliaments were formed. In a 1983 survey, about 40 percent of German local communities had some form of advisory council for a total number of about three hundred groups. In France consultative institutions existed in some municipalities since 1971. At the national level, the Conseil National des Populations was established by the Ministry of Labor in 1984. However, foreigners in France did not have a right of association until 1981. (Interestingly, in that same year, France recognized the right of individual petition, under Article 25 of the ECHR—see chap. 4.) Instead, "solidarity associations," established by French nationals to which immigrants could be affiliated, represented migrant interests. Consultation took the form of informal commissions where such associations could raise migrant problems at the local level. After 1981, the foreign workers and residents formed their own associations.[78]

Migrant links to political, civic, church, and humanitarian organizations have further helped their cause. In France, left-wing parties competed to proclaim the support for foreign workers. In Germany, foreign workers constituted several thousand of the Social Democratic Party's (SPD) members. In both countries major religious bodies have taken positions in favor of the migrants and in publicizing foreigners' grievances. The migrants themselves have taken the initiative to push church councils and lay organizations to promote migrant interests. Humanitarian groups, such as the Fédération des Associations de Solidarité avec les Travailleurs Immigrés (FASTI) have publicized worker grievances. Civil rights groups, such as the Movement against Racism, Anti-Semitism and for Peace (MRAP), have combated racism directed against the migrants.[79]

It is striking how, even in countries where there are strong ties between the state and corporate bodies, transnational ties between migrants and those corporate bodies can develop that do not necessarily overlap with the interest of the state. This takes place, it should be stressed, after the legal entry of the migrants. So the "transnational alliance" is less likely to have developed if the migrants were not allowed entry in the first place, in contrast to the U.S. case.

The failure in regulation, to reiterate, took place domestically, not at the border. In Germany, for example, welfare and church organizations put themselves at the service of the state in helping migrants, as temporary workers, adjust to an unfamiliar environment. But having developed links with the migrants, and seeing their presence had political, social, and cultural dimensions (and not just economic), these welfare and church organizations began to act politically for the migrants from the early 1970s. They lobbied for education for migrant children, improved residential rights, and political participation rights, among other issues.[80] Whereas at first they acted hand in hand with the state authorities, they later shifted into an adversarial and advocacy role.

Ties between employers and migrants proved, of course, a critical element in anchoring the foreign workers into their host societies. In this regard, the ties may have had more of a contractual (as opposed to an affective) character, but the segmentation of the labor market made the migrants an essential resource to the employers. For the segmented market, itself a product of the guest-worker program, not having the foreign workers would have led to a shortage of workers in certain sectors. This, in turn, would force up wages. Severe economic dislocation in industries such as construction and automobile assembly would have followed the loss of the foreign labor.[81]

In addition to the domestic constituencies that acted on behalf of the migrants after their entry, the foreign workers were actively represented by their home governments. Such representation was a function of the bilateral treaties that facilitated the initial entry of guest workers. The foreign workers' diplomatic representatives intervened in issues that ranged from labor conflicts to local elections. Homeland fraternal organizations were subsidized and supported by home governments in their efforts to aid (and, in certain cases, spy upon) the migrants. Home governments sent clergy and teachers and sponsored television and radio shows to promote homeland identification. Curiously, migrants thus had political channels not available to the native population.[82]

With the multifarious links that developed, and the ethnic "exclaves" that mushroomed with migration, we have, in a number of senses, countries "whose boundaries are not delimited." The diplomatic representation, however, could not be responsible for the full range of migrant concerns. Instead the foreign workers turned to increasing involvement in domestic politics. The ties that were spun between migrants' host governments, home governments, and indigenous populations transformed classic conceptions of interstate relations. Now nongovernmental associations from one society could influence politics in another society, bypassing the governments concerned altogether.[83]

The economic rationale of international migration breaks down with family reunification and permanent settlement. At that point, foreign labor ceases to be a commodity that is easily exchanged and disposed of, and ceases to be significantly cheaper than indigenous labor. As settlers, the "foreign workers" make demands on various social services, including unemployment support, housing, schools, and, eventually, pensions. Germany and France, among other countries, would attempt to halt the importation of additional migrants in 1973–74. But they failed to "rotate" the foreign workers on a massive scale back to their homelands. Family reunification—the indisputable sign of permanent settlement—accelerated dramatically. It is by family reunification that regulatory attempts were ultimately broken. The links, the multitudinous "private" transnational ties between the migrants and the indigenous unions, civic and church groups, and the employers overcame the states' attempts at control.

One may expect France, with its centralized administration, which is relatively immune to pressure groups, to have had an easier time of implementing restrictions. But in Germany, interest groups are more closely linked to the state, and policies could be more easily coordinated. French employers' associations lobbied for exemptions to the restrictions on importing foreign labor. The German employers supported their government—so long as they could rely on the additional labor provided by family immigration. Trade unions in both countries supported policies on regaining control on migration but sought to integrate those foreign workers (with the concomitant family unification) already resident in the respective countries. Civic, humanitarian, and church groups pressured their governments to lift limits on family reunification. This was particularly true in Germany, where the rules on uniting families were stricter. But, as noted earlier, the net effect of policy differences between the two countries was the impact on the time lag of the phases of immigration, not on the process itself.[84] Family reunification accelerated foreign population growth even though labor importation was halted. The ties between migrant and indigenous groups undermined immigration policy. In such circumstances, mass expulsion was unthinkable. It is striking that state and society could cooperate on halting further migration at the border, but even in Germany, the ties of employers, unions, and civic groups with resident foreign workers overcame the traditional national pact between state and nation.

Attention turned in Western European countries instead to integrating the foreign workers into their societies. The migrants had become settlers. The focus shifted from the migrants as purely economic actors, to questions of civil and political rights and their place in the respective societies. The migrants, in turn, sought "social justice" and fair treatment for themselves and their families without compromising their national and religious affiliations.[85] They too would adopt the idiom and institutions of international human rights to further their cause.[86] Citizenship, as the exclusive principle defining membership in the state and the linchpin of the nation-state, came under challenge.

Migrant Rights and the Value of Citizenship

Since 1973, with the decision to integrate already resident migrants into their host societies, European states have introduced legislation to ensure the rights and status of migrants and their families. Well over half of the foreign populations are now legally permanent residents. Even in Germany, 69 percent of the foreigners had permanent residency status by 1986. Since the 1980s, political and civil rights have been progressively extended to the foreign populations. Indeed, the membership status and rights of resident foreigners have reached the point where the distinction between citizen and noncitizen is not very significant.[87]

In the area of social services—such as education, health insurance, welfare, and unemployment benefits—citizenship status is of minor importance. Physical presence and legal alien status are the determining criteria. Family allowances are available for children of migrants who live outside the host country. Most countries will pay retirement benefits even if the migrants return to their home country. Legal alien permanent residents can, in almost all cases, legally take up employment or start their own businesses. In this respect, they have the same status as citizens, except in the civil service and in professions where loyalty to the state is deemed necessary. However, even in the civil service, aliens are making inroads in certain countries through admission to police, military, and other civil service positions.[88]

Aliens are guaranteed full civil rights, either constitutionally or by statute. The German Basic Law and the Belgian constitution recognize citizens and noncitizens alike as carriers of most rights and freedoms. Aliens may acquire property just like nationals, except in Sweden.[89]

In the political arena, citizenship is essential for voting in national elections. Since 1973, local voting rights have been extended to noncitizens in a number of countries. In Germany, the Federal Constitutional Court rejected local voting rights for aliens in 1990 on constitutional grounds. The issue of local voting rights is under debate in France and Belgium. Some parties in the Netherlands and Sweden (where foreign residents do have local voting rights) advocate national voting rights for aliens. The main avenues for alien political representation continue to be the alien assemblies and consultative councils.[90] Even in those countries that have more readily extended local voting rights to foreign residents, there has been a reluctance to extend national voting rights to such persons. The civic and even nationalist symbolism of parliamentary elections is, it appears, the final bastion and expression of nationhood.[91]

Aliens can also form or join organizations and parties to advance their collective interests. This was by no means always the case. France, as noted earlier, allowed foreigners to form associations only in 1981. In Germany, in contrast, foreign residents could demonstrate and attend assemblies in 1953 and form their own associations in 1964. By 1967 they could join political parties.[92]

The effect of the disappearing distinction between citizen and alien is that resident aliens display little interest in citizenship status. Thus citizenship, in the host countries, is devalued. This is exemplified by the low propensity of resident aliens, in Europe as in the United States, to naturalize. The low rate of naturalization is only partly a function of the stringency of the requirements; many aliens do not request citizenship even when they have the option. When more than half of the foreigners in Europe have spent the requisite time as residents to claim citizenship, we find naturalization rates (relative to the size of the foreign population) for the year of 1980 of, at best, 5 percent in Sweden to, at worst, 0.3 percent in Germany.[93] The differences in naturalization rates are significant and do highlight political and cultural differences noted earlier in comparing French and German concepts of nationhood; equally significant, however, is that in *every* Western country naturalization rates, or interest in naturalizing among resident aliens, is low.[94]

In a 1985 survey, when more than 70 percent of the foreign population resident in Germany was eligible for naturalization, only 6.2 percent expressed an intention to seek German citizenship. Most (40 percent) stated that they wanted to remain citizens of their home country. Others (14 percent) did not want to lose their native citizenship that naturalization in Germany would entail. Another 7 percent disliked "the German way of life." Naturalization, notes Tomas Hammar, is not perceived as a formality; it "presupposes a profound transformation of the applicant [such that] his ties to the old country are broken and that he intends to stay for the rest of his life in [the host country]."[95]

The primary reasons why citizenship has been devalued lies in the ex post facto character of migrant membership. The migrants never went through formal immigration procedures or ritual. Second, the migrants had to be legally recognized but the host countries, especially Germany, were at best ambivalent about absorbing the migrants. The effect was to create a set of rights for the migrant almost equal to the rights of a citizen and thus there has been little incentive to naturalize. Third, and in a broader sense, the continuity of national self-definition, of nationhood, has been compromised, if not broken. This is particularly true for Germany with its *volkisch*, ethnonational self-definition. But it is also true for France, with its traditional stress on "assimilable" aliens and the franco-politicization of immigrants. The migrants have not, in many cases, assimilated into Frenchmen in any traditional sense as symbolized in, for example, the furor over the refusal of Muslim girls to remove their headscarves in French public schools.[96]

Because the U.S. failure to control transnational migration was primarily at the border and not, as in the Western European case, a domestic failure, the analytical focus shifts. We have to consider the institutional factors, such as the role of interest groups and the federal government, and the ideological factors that impeded border control. Furthermore, U.S. efforts to halt or substantially reduce illegal immigration come to be focused in specific legislation, most importantly the Immigration Reform and Control Act of 1986. That legislation must, consequently, play a central role in any analysis of the U.S. attempts to regulate transnational migration. In contrast, the process of trying to rotate guest workers out of their host countries in Western Europe, as well as the progressive integration of the migrants into their host countries, was a lengthier one.

3

Immigration and Citizenship
in the United States

THE IMMIGRATION REFORM AND
CONTROL ACT OF 1986

After a flat period of more then forty years, immigration to the United States increased dramatically following the amendments to the immigration laws of 1965. The 1965 amendments gave strong preference to family reunification, permitting a rise to historically high rates of immigration (more than 973,000 legal immigrants in fiscal 1992). The family reunification focus of the amendments also led to a change in the ethnic makeup of the immigrants, with more Asians and Latin Americans coming in than Europeans. Immigrants were thus not only greater in number than at any time since the early 1920s, demographers point out, but they were more noticeable.[1]

In this same period, the number of illegal aliens ballooned as a result of regional and global economic changes. By fiscal 1988, illegal aliens were settling in the country at an estimated rate of 200,000 persons per year. The growing population of illegal aliens, together with dramatic increases in the number coming in under refugee quotas, gave rise to a pervasive sense that the United States had "lost control of its borders." The Select Commission on Immigration and Refugee Policy, established by Congress in 1978, identified illegal migration as an urgent problem.[2]

In 1986 Congress passed the Immigration Reform and Control Act (IRCA). IRCA brought about major changes in U.S. immigration law. It included several provisions designed to combat illegal entry into the country. These provisions included a legalization program for certain illegal aliens already in the country, sanctions against employers who hired illegal aliens, increased border enforcement, and a program allowing aliens to be employed as temporary agricultural workers. Legal immigration policies were, for the most part, left untouched.[3] IRCA is significant because it illustrates an attempt—indeed, *the* major attempt—to assert American sovereignty in the face of external events and pressures. IRCA also demonstrates how, in tandem with other legal developments, migratory pressures are affecting distinctions between citizen and alien.

This chapter examines why the United States has been unable to significantly and enduringly contain illegal migration. The U.S. failure will be increasingly critical for the value of citizenship; concomitant with the loosening of state-society ties that the loss of state control implies, transnational linkages take on an increasing importance.[4] Lobbying groups that are hostile to restrictive controls on immigration, particularly ethnic and business interests, blunt the effectiveness of attempts to legislate and implement laws on ending illegal immigration. Laws such as IRCA consequently become, in the words of Congressman Romano Mazzoli, a "delicate balance of interests," a balance that dilutes the state's efforts to control illegal entry. The potency of the lobbyists is a function of certain historical developments. Ethnic and ideological parameters, limiting who could become a member of this country, have eroded or disappeared. This development, in turn, has widened the claims that interest groups can make in the area of immigration. Groups, such as the Hispanics, who were once marginalized and relatively small in number (prior to, in particular, the abolition of ethnic quotas in 1965), now can make much greater demands of the political center. A primarily Anglo society in the 1950s, for example, tolerated mass deportations of illegal Mexican aliens. Such a move today would be considered illegitimate and politically inadvisable, to put it mildly. The historical and normative changes will be described and documented in this chapter.

Although IRCA was partially successful in the first two years, when illegal entry was reduced by some 35 percent as a result of the law, IRCA did not fully reestablish the state's role of determining membership in U.S. society. Part of the IRCA package was to legalize retroactively the residency of more than three million illegal entrants to the country. In effect, membership in this society was established on the grounds of the actual social and economic links such aliens had with Americans, also known as "membership by proxy," rather than membership through the channels of the sovereign state.[5] Although the *principle* of membership by proxy was not recognized, the limited success of IRCA and the precedent of retroactive legalization will force a more permanent institutionalization of some principle of membership by proxy. Finally, given the now equivocal character of American national identity, legislation on immigration has and increasingly will turn to transnational, universal, and "neutral" criteria, as opposed to national and state-centric criteria, for defining who may immigrate and become members of this society (see, for example, the subsequent discussion of the Refugee Act of 1980, which incorporates a U.N. definition of what constitutes a refugee). In sum, transnational relations are becoming increasingly legitimate. The state's role and character are being altered.

In the classic paradigm, it falls upon the state, as the sovereign and representative body, to mediate who may enter and who may be naturalized. The sovereign status of the state is so central in such circumstances that immigration law in the United States has, up to now, been relatively insulated from constitutional limitations. Immigration law, Peter Schuck notes, "remains the realm in which government authority is at the zenith, and individual entitlement is at the nadir." The courts have shown great deference to the other branches of government in the area of immigration, much in the way the courts have been circumspect in asserting their opinions in the area of foreign policy.[6] Insofar as the state defines criteria as to who may enter the country, the state is implicitly (and not always consciously) making a statement about its place in the world. Nationality laws, ethnic preferences, and ideological affinities, when used to categorize potential immigrants, are indicators of the state's attitudes in the international arena as much as an expression of how it wishes domestic society to be constituted. In the United States in particular, immigration policies have historically reflected the country's foreign politics.

Historical Background

Only after the Civil War does an unambiguously *national* society (as opposed to a community based on the individual states) emerge in the United States. The regulation and naturalization of aliens prior to the late nineteenth century was considered a state, not a federal, issue.[7] Congress required, in a law passed in 1790, that the states perform naturalization procedures, but naturalized citizens were considered to be members of the national community, which transcended the states. Rights and duties stemming from citizenship in one state were enforced by the courts in all the states. The delegates to the Constitutional Congress failed to clarify the relationship between state and national citizenship and, similarly, failed to determine what was the primary locus of the citizen's loyalties. The courts also skirted the issue. Only the slavery issue and the Civil War would force a resolution as to who are "the people" and where their primary allegiances lay. Prior to this period immigration into the United States was unregulated. By 1875, the regulation (and, in certain cases, the exclusion) of immigrants became a federal concern.[8]

This is not to say, however, that the concept of citizenship was not important in the earlier historical period. The Revolution, Peter Schuck and Rogers Smith point out, was not merely the transfer of loyalties from one sovereign to another. The Revolution fashioned, or sought to fashion, a nation. This new nation was legitimated through the aggregate of the individual citizens' consent, which replaced the passive and imputed allegiance of subjects to the Crown.[9] The creation of a new citizenship was thus at the heart of the Revolution. What is striking about this concept of citizenship, radical for its time, was that it created terms for membership and, by implication, created the category of aliens. Early English law made no distinction between subject and alien. A continuum of ranks and rights characterized society, not members and nonmembers. In the seventeenth century, with the rise of national states, the concept of the alien arose, but the older ideas lingered.[10] The American Revolution caused a break with traditional practice.

The consensual character of citizenship is one of the enduring contributions of the Revolution. The principle of consent, to a lesser or greater degree accepted by all states following the Revolution, demands that political membership be a function of individual choice. In 1776 the revolutionaries rejected the claim that allegiance was perpetual or simply a function of an objective circumstance, such as birth within a certain sovereign's jurisdiction. Allegiance was contractual and such allegiance could be annulled, as the colonies had chosen to annul their supposed fealty to Britain. Americans after 1776 believed that every man had the right to choose his status, whether to be a citizen or an alien. Both Federalists and Republicans suggested that immigrants should be of a certain *political* character, although they could not agree on precisely what the parameters of that character should be.[11] (The Federalist faction took the notion that immigrants should be of a certain political character to an extreme when they put through the Alien Sedition Act in 1798. It was designed to keep out immigrants who, it was feared, would become Republicans. It was overturned two years later.)

This consensual understanding of citizenship highlights what Yehoshua Arieli has referred to as the coincidence of the political and the national revolution; the political identity (broadly expressed in the Constitution) was the American identity. That identity was not so much a function of one's bloodline (with, of course, the fundamental exceptions of black and native Americans) as a function of ideas, of ideology.[12] Conversely, an alien was one who rejected the premises underlying American nationhood. This concept of citizenship makes the line between citizen and alien rather permeable (although ideological lines can be drawn more or less sharply). The permeability of the distinction between citizen and alien is apparent in the Constitution, which confers rights on "persons" or "people" and not on citizens per se. Entry into the United States, as a consequence, has historically been relatively easy. Prior to the Civil War immigration was largely unregulated.[13] With some variations between states, naturalization was available to all whites who fulfilled the residency requirement and took an oath of loyalty.[14]

The ideological character of American citizenship was also reflected in the idea of the United States as an "asylum" and in the belief that anybody can be assimilated into American society. However, the belief that values define the citizen also meant that those values or the "quality" of the potential immigrant was always open to negotiation. This became all the more apparent as the federal government began, in the late nineteenth century, to define who would be eligible to enter the country.[15]

In the 1840s immigration began to grow substantially. In that decade almost two million persons immigrated, and there was a steady increase in immigrant arrivals for the next six decades, except during the Civil War and the economic depression of the 1890s. Immigration reached unprecedented levels in the 1880s, attaining a figure of five million persons. Immigration peaked in the first decade of this century at nine million immigrants. The proportion of the population that was foreign-born in 1910 was nearly 15 percent. (Compare to the percentage of foreign-born in 1980, at little more than 6 percent.)[16]

After the Union's victory in the Civil War established the central government as the object of primary allegiance, the federal government began to assume its role as the regulator of immigration. Already in 1864 Congress passed a bill establishing a Bureau of Immigration to keep records. In 1875 the Supreme Court determined that Congress had the role of regulating immigration and that all state immigration laws then existing were unconstitutional.[17]

Various laws were passed from 1875 through to 1917 excluding certain categories of immigrants such as felons, "lunatics and idiots," and anarchists. Racial exclusion made its appearance in 1882 in the Chinese Exclusion Law. Congress suspended the entry of Chinese immigrants and forbade naturalization of all foreign-born Chinese.[18]

The Immigration Act of 1917 and the Immigration Act of 1924 were the first laws to place numerical and ethnic limits on entrants. The 1917 act had a literacy requirement, which, in effect, placed a numerical limit on immigrants and, furthermore, discriminated against immigrants from southern and eastern Europe where illiteracy was high. Proponents of the act believed that the literacy test would decrease the number of immigrants from those regions by 25 percent.[19]

In fact there was only a slight dip in immigration; 805,000 immigrants arrived in 1921, which was comparable with some pre–World War I figures.[20] The 1924 act (like a temporary act in 1921) sought to accomplish the same goals of numerical limitation and ethnic selection more directly. The 1921 law established the quota system by which immigration was limited to 3 percent of the number of foreign-born of each European ethnic group present in the country at the 1910 census, a rule that favored northern European immigrants.[21]

The 1921 restrictions were apparently motivated by fears of an onrush of immigrants, a "barbarian horde" heading westward after World War I. Fears that Bolshevik aliens would enter the country were a factor. The proponents of the 1924 quotas were more explicitly racist. They cited the importance of racial homogeneity and claims of Anglo-Saxon superiority, while attacking arguments for the melting pot as fallacious. They warned of "racial indigestion."[22]

The 1924 act established a yearly quota of 150,000 for the European countries, to be divided according to the proportion of foreign-born residents in the United States in 1890. The use of the 1890 census discriminated against southern and eastern Europeans even more than the earlier quotas based on the 1910 census. The 1924 law ended the immigration of aliens ineligible for naturalization, including the Chinese and the Japanese. In due course, further legislation in 1927 replaced the quotas based on the 1890 census with the national origins plan which used the 1920 census as a base.[23]

Only minor changes were made to the rules for exclusion, with the exception of legislation on subversives, from 1924 to 1952.[24] Immigration during the period of the Depression and World War II was very low—less then 50,000 entrants per year from 1932 to 1945.[25] One important development following the war was the creation of a special immigration status for refugees. At President Truman's initiative, bills were passed to absorb some of the "displaced persons" resulting from the war in Europe. In part this was an attempt to bolster Western Europe in the West's struggle against the Soviet Union.[26]

Soon after World War II immigration categories again took on an ideological color. Foreign politics had assumed a Manichaean quality, and international relations were projected as a bipolar struggle between the free world and communism. National boundaries became less significant, from the American perspective, than the division dividing East from West. Immigration law came to reflect that outlook. National origins quotas were initially retained, but their incongruence became increasingly apparent.

The Immigration and Nationality Act of 1952, known as the McCarran-Walter Act, revised, codified, and repealed nearly all existing immigration law. The law was enacted at height of the cold war, during the Korean War, and while Stalin was still in power. This law incorporated the Internal Security Act of 1950, which mentioned the Communist Party for the first time by name, provided for the exclusion of Communist Party members, "fellow travellers," and supporters of the doctrine of "world communism." This was amended slightly in 1952, so that persons who had been forced to join the Communist Party in foreign countries or defectors would not be excluded. The act retained the national origins quotas with some modifications. Asian countries were allocated small immigration quotas. This allocation reflected concern that Asian countries should not be alienated during the conflict with Communist countries. Quotas in general were justified, as the Senate Judiciary Committee put it, without "giving credence to any theory of Nordic superiority," but in order to preserve the "sociological and cultural balance" in the United States.[27] The act also introduced a quota preference for immigrants with skills.

The category of "alien" took on a primarily ideological, as opposed to an ethnic, association. Alien *beliefs*, not nationalities, were now the focus of concern. During hearings on the McCarran-Walter bill in 1949, for example, ex-Communist witnesses were brought forward to testify that the real control of the Communist Party in the United States was in the hands of foreign aliens who came and left the country as they pleased. Aliens holding these foreign beliefs, it was said, could not be allowed in to subvert the country: "We must bring our immigration system into line with the realities of communist tactics," Senator McCarran asserted.[28] (Conversely, as Samuel Huntington has pointed out, "American" was the way of life poised in opposition to communism, as suggested in the title of the congressional committee designed to investigate "Un-American activities.")[29]

The retention of national origins quotas was in contradiction, as already noted, with the ideological thrust of the 1952 act. Quotas alienated nationalities whose support was needed in the overriding struggle with communism. The public debates over the debilitating effect, as far as foreign policy was concerned, of ethnic quotas ultimately led to the abolition of ethnically discriminatory quotas in 1965. The objections to the quotas were expressed by President Truman's veto (subsequently overridden) of the McCarran-Walters bill. Truman's objections captured the new sense of how American nationality was to be defined:

> The basis of this quota system was false and unworthy in 1924. It is even worse now. At the present time this quota system keeps out the very people we want to bring in. It is incredible to me that, in this year of 1952, we should be enacting into law such a slur on the patriotism and the decency of a large part of our citizenry.
>
> Today we have entered into an alliance . . . with Italy, Greece, and Turkey against one of the most terrible threats mankind has ever faced. . . . But, through this bill we say to their people: You are less worthy to come this country than Englishmen or Irishmen. . . .
>
> Today we are "protecting" ourselves as we were in 1924, against being flooded by immigrants from Eastern Europe. This is fantastic. The countries of Eastern Europe have fallen under the Communist yoke—they are silenced, fenced off by barbed wire and minefields—no one passes their borders but at the risk of his life. We do not need to be protected against immigrants from these countries—on the contrary we want to stretch out a helping hand, to save those who have managed to flee into Western Europe, to succor those who are brave enough to escape from barbarism, to welcome and restore them against the day when their countries will, as we hope, be free again. . . . These are a few examples of the absurdity, the

cruelty of carrying over into this year of 1952 the isolationist limitations of our 1924 law.

In no other realm of our national life are we so hampered and stultified by the dead hand of the past, as we are in this field of immigration.[30]

Immigration and refugee policy up to 1965 continued to be character-ized by tension between the national origins restrictions and the apparent need for admitting refugees from Communist countries and a humanitar-ian desire to unite families. Temporary programs were enacted in order to bypass the oversubscribed quotas and to provide for nonquota admission of foreigners, especially refugees. Recognition by many congressmen that the national origins quotas were dysfunctional for American foreign policy paved the way for major revisions in immigration law. President Kennedy, calling the quotas an "anachronism" that discriminated on the basis of "accident of birth," submitted to Congress proposals for repeal-ing the national origins quota system.[31]

The Immigration and Nationality Act of 1965 indeed repealed the national origins quota system. However, the ideological and security provisions of the 1952 act remained in force. Limits were placed on the number of immigrants that could arrive from the Western and Eastern Hemispheres respectively, and from each country in the Eastern Hemi-sphere. Within these numerical limits, visas were available according to a seven-level preference system. This system placed family reunification as the first priority, over that of the need to attract skilled and professional persons. Thus, by asserting a kinship principle in immigration law, there was some continuity with the ethnic criteria of old. In this respect the law was a compromise and many favoring the change, including Attorney General Robert Kennedy, did not believe it would alter the ethnic compo-sition of the United States. In other words, formal discrimination was ended but opponents of the change were mollified by the belief that the country would, in its ethnic proportions, remain unchanged. It was believed that family reunification would simply draw in immigrants from the parent countries of present citizens.[32]

They were, of course, fundamentally mistaken. The politicians did not foresee the family preference's potential for chain migration. The Asian-American population was less then 1 percent of the U.S. total in 1960. Asian immigration would change that radically.[33] The politics of immigra-tion had been changed forever. Lobbying groups represented a multiplic-ity of ethnic groups and interests, with no single group dominant, as became evident in the IRCA case. There was no going back to national quotas. Ideological criteria for immigration remained intact but later these too would come under attack. With the passage of the Immigration Act of 1990, ideological criteria become marginal. The problem of illegal aliens would in time grow dramatically in the consciousness of the American public. National borders, communal boundaries, and the distinction between citizen and alien were, it appeared, becoming hazy. By the mid-1970s, calls were made to bring the borders under control.

Thus a pattern of immigration legislation following large influxes of foreigners is apparent, first in the 1920s and then following World War II.[34] Beginning early in the twentieth century, two sets of criteria for immigration are evident, ethnic and ideological criteria respectively. By 1952, utilitarian criteria—professional and skilled labor qualifications— appear, though they are of secondary importance at the time. Although ethnic and ideological "qualifications" are demanded of potential immigrants throughout this period, it is evident that ethnic categories dominate the immigrant admission process from 1917 to World War II, and ideological tests are predominant in the postwar period.

An ethnic basis to immigration laws makes for a strongly defined distinction between citizen and alien. For a nation-state where a group of one national origin forms a substantial majority of its citizens, the issue of restrictions and preferences for that national group in immigration law is not likely to be problematic and is considered a simple practice of self-determination. Germany is a country that heavily favors those of German ethnic descent. In the multiethnic United States, however, such an approach proved to be problematic. The national origins quota system had the effect of, as Robert Divine puts it, producing competition in immigration matters among the various ethnic groups in the United States. Each minority demanded a larger quota for its own nationality of origin. Competitive bidding ensued, which led to factionalism rather than national unity.[35] The parameters of debate about what constituted a "desirable" immigrant, however, still focused on those of European ancestry— the question was whether more southern and eastern Europeans should be allowed in. The exclusion of Japanese and Chinese produced little national controversy in this period. In the longer term, and under the pressure of international politics, the system of discriminatory ethnic quotas had to be downgraded and then dropped.

Ideological distinctions drawn from international conflict tend to blur national boundaries because ideology, being universally propagated and claiming universal application, is not tied to a specific territory the way a national ethnic group may be. This blurring of boundaries was compounded by the until recently bipolar conception of American foreign politics. The political connotation of "alien" stresses the alien ideology. Furthermore, ideological definitions of membership are always negotiable. Ideological distinctions do not have the clarity or apparently fixed nature of national (ethnic) criteria for immigration. Indeed, ideological definitions of the national community are being "negotiated" almost out of existence. New utilitarian criteria are being put forward to define desirable immigrants and, in turn, citizens.

These issues become secondary, however, in the face of massive illegal migration. If illegal entry cannot be stopped or substantially impeded, then the citizen-alien distinction becomes moot. The erosion of ethnic and ideological criteria changed the dynamics of interest group politics on the question of illegal immigration. Broader claims on the political center could be made, and state control could be more easily blunted.

Immigration Reform

Since the turn of the century Mexicans have migrated north to the United States to work on the railroads and in the rapidly expanding agricultural business in the Southwest. Restrictions on entry imposed in 1917 remained, in practical terms, unenforced. Employers were legally able and eager to hire from this pool of cheap labor. Provisos, added to the 1917 immigration law under pressure from agricultural and railroad interests, allowed the entry of temporary workers. This program terminated in 1923, but the illegal flow of temporary workers back and forth across the Mexican border continued. The Depression brought this migration to a close, when hundreds of thousands of Mexicans were repatriated.[36]

American participation in World War II, and the consequent diversion of labor to the war effort, brought about an arrangement in 1942 between the United States and Mexico for the legal entry of temporary agricultural workers, the *braceros*. The bracero program, initially an emergency wartime measure, lasted under different legal authorizations for twenty-two years and involved roughly five million Mexicans. The employment of Mexican workers in the 1950s under this program was considerably more extensive then it had been during the wartime years. Paradoxically, the bracero program, together with economic developments in the region, gave a strong impetus to illegal entry into the United States. The upward jump in illegal immigration began in 1944, two years after the program's inception. Apprehension figures of deportable aliens from 1944–54 suggest that illegal entry was very high, comparable with the level of the early 1970s, though lower than in the 1980s. Apparently, contract workers returned to Mexico with descriptions of the work opportunities in the United States, inspiring others to journey northward.[37]

In the late 1950s the bracero program came under increasing attack from labor groups who claimed that the Mexican temporary workers were adversely affecting the wages and working conditions of domestic workers in certain areas and occupations. Under this pressure, the legal importation of temporary workers was finally suspended in 1964.[38]

After the suspension of the program, illegal migration jumped dramatically. Apprehensions increased from under 87,000 in 1964 to more than 280,000 in 1969. Apprehensions jumped dramatically in the 1970s, reaching a historical high of 8.3 million for the decade. By the late 1970s and early 1980s the Immigration Service (INS) was apprehending about 1 million persons annually, peaking in 1986 at 1.8 million. Light industries, as well as farm work, were now drawing on these migrants for cheap labor.[39]

Net immigration—the number of immigrants less emigrants, calculated as a proportion of the population—has reached nothing like the level of the late nineteenth or early twentieth centuries. Passel and Woodrow note that net immigration accounted for 4.1 percent of the population, and 30 percent of the population growth from 1900 to 1910. After dropping to a net immigration rate of almost zero in the Depression, net immigration grew to 1.3–1.4 percent in 1950 and has remained at a fairly constant level until recently. So why did immigration receive so much attention in the 1980s in the media and in government? Demographic factors are cited: a dramatic change in the ethnic composition of the immigrants and the increasing importance of immigration, relative to births, as a factor in population growth. In 1980, the proportion of foreign-born grew for the first time in sixty years, reaching 6.2 percent, or 1 person in every 16. Finally, immigration attained prominence as an issue because of the undocumented population.[40] It is the illegal immigrants who primarily account for the increased current interest in immigration issues. The changing demographic composition of the country may have helped draw attention to the problem of the illegal immigrants. For the public at large, as well as for policymakers, the issue came to be seen as a need to reestablish control of the nation's borders and, in essence, to reassert national sovereignty.[41]

The timing of the debate followed the massive jump in illegal immigration that took place in the 1970s and the 1980s. A number of estimates have been offered on the size of the illegal population, an obviously difficult population to count, but the calculations based on census data appear to be the most reliable. From studies of the 1980 census and INS data sources, demographers estimate that there were 2.5 to 3.5 million illegal aliens in the country at the time of the census. Of the undocumented migrants counted in the 1980 census, 26 percent entered before 1970, 28 percent during 1970–74, and 46 percent during 1975–80. Mexicans represented 55 percent of this group. These figures only relate to those present in 1980, so it is possible, as Passel and Woodrow point out, that the rise in illegal residents suggested by these figures is illusionary.[42] Many earlier immigrants (prior to 1970, say) may have subsequently emigrated prior to the 1980 census. However, data on apprehensions, cited earlier, suggest that a dramatic rise in the number of illegal entries in the 1970s and in the 1980s did indeed occur.

Illegal migration was (and is) driven largely by labor pressures in the Caribbean Basin, and by the need of U.S. employers for low-skill, low-wage labor, a need that is compounded by the shortage of legal workers as the "baby bust" generation enters the labor market. The Caribbean Basin's population of 164 million in 1980 was three-quarters that of the United States. By the turn of the century, that population is expected to draw even with that of the United States, at 275 million. Projections for the year 2025 estimate that the basin will have a population 25 percent larger than that of the United States (372 million compared with 301 million). The labor force in the basin, 53 million strong in 1980, is projected to be 150 million by the year 2025. If the ceiling on unemployment *rates* in the basin is to be maintained at 1980 levels to the year 2010, Thomas Espenshade and his colleagues write, more than 7 million extra jobs would have to be created at an added cost of $270 billion (in 1982 dollars). (To meet this goal, between 40 and 50 percent of that investment was due by the end of the 1980s, an investment that did not occur.) Eighty percent of the investment is needed in Mexico and the Caribbean Islands. If investment on these levels is not forthcoming, the pressures arising from unemployment are likely to grow in the next decade, including pressures for undocumented migration. This pressure is likely to peak, what's more, when the need for foreign workers in the United States is at its greatest, due to the expected domestic shortfall in the supply of unskilled entry-level workers in many industrial categories.[43]

One must add the proviso, however, that other developments can alter the picture; an ongoing recession in the United States, for example, may depress the attraction of undocumented migration. The impact of the North American Free Trade Agreement (NAFTA) is also in question: it is suggested by some analysts that NAFTA will produce an initial migratory push into the American labor market but that overall migration will subside if jobs sought by migrants shift to Mexico.[44]

LEGISLATIVE HISTORY OF IRCA:
"THE DELICATE BALANCE OF INTERESTS"

By the early 1970s the problem of illegal immigration became an active issue in Washington. The actual number of illegal aliens was a matter of speculation at this time but public attitudes to the phenomenon were clearly hostile.[45] Public opinion hardened further as other immigration issues arose. Particularly exacerbating was the influx of Vietnamese refugees after 1975, reaching a peak of 14,000 a month in 1979; the 1980 Cuban Mariel refugees, who numbered 125,000; and the Central American refugees, who entered throughout the 1980s.[46] Over this period, from the introduction of a bill in 1971 under the sponsorship of Representative Peter Rodino until IRCA was passed in 1986, Congress debated the issue of illegal immigration. From the beginning, employer sanctions—that is, penalizing employers who hire illegal aliens—were the core of the legislative attempts to stem illegal immigration. The lengthy period it took to pass IRCA was largely a function satisfying the different interests concerned with this bill. To win the support of the interest groups involved, concessions were made, from the retroactive legalization of undocumented aliens already living in this country to the temporary-worker programs and the creation of a special office to ensure discrimination would not be a byproduct of IRCA. These concessions, however, also compromised the effectiveness of attempts to control undocumented migration.

That Congress acted on a bill restricting the entry of illegal aliens was, Harris Miller points out, remarkable.[47] Immigration is believed to be a "no-win" issue for most congressmen. Immigration legislation is generally of a restrictive nature. Most interest groups interested in immigration, particularly ethnic and agricultural interests, are against restrictions, especially restrictions against illegal aliens. A majority of the American public is hostile to liberal immigration measures in general and against illegal immigration in particular, but it is not organized to act on that sentiment.[48]

This accounts for the legislature's slow response to the illegal entry problem, graphically exemplified by the reluctance, until IRCA, to impose penalties on those who hire illegal aliens. This sensitivity to the interests of the employers was made explicit when a proviso added to the McCarran-Walter Act in 1952 declared that the employment of aliens was not "harboring," an offense under the 1952 act. McCarran referred to legal impediments to illegal entry from Mexico as "red tape" at the very time he was promoting restrictive immigration legislation.[49] Thus, for the alien, employment is available in the United States, entry is relatively easy because of limited border enforcement (until recently at least), the penalty for being caught is mild, and economic conditions at home are very bad.[50]

The resolve of Congress to act on the illegal alien problem when it became particularly serious in the early 1970s derived from a common concern about controlling the borders. The resolution to do something had to overcome the opposition of a constellation of interest groups. Concessions were necessary to at least partially alleviate the concerns of the major interest groups.

Rodino succeeded in introducing, and having the House pass overwhelmingly on two occasions, in 1971 and in 1972, a bill against hiring illegal aliens. However, the bill was opposed by farming interests and spokesmen said to represent Hispanic-Americans who feared that the employer sanctions would lead to discrimination against Hispanics. The agricultural business lobby succeeded in bottling the bill up in the Senate Judiciary committee through the support of the Committee chair, Senator James Eastland. In the mid-1970s Rodino tied employer sanctions to a plan for legalization of illegal aliens who were already residing in the United States. It was thought that legalization was the only practical and humane way of dealing with the millions of illegal residents. Furthermore, it would appeal to the major interests involved. Employers would not lose long-term employees illegally in the country. The Hispanic community favored the plan. This proposal was not acted upon in 1975. In 1977, the Carter administration put forward a similar program, but at this point supporters of immigration reform had despaired, and the proposal was not acted upon. Finally, in 1978, Congress established a Select Commission on Immigration and Refugee Policy to produce legislative recommendations.[51]

The commission, headed by Reverend Theodore Hesburgh, submitted its final report, entitled *U.S. Immigration Policy and the National Interest*, on March 1, 1981. The commission highlighted the problem of defining boundaries in a country where such distinctions were becoming less and less clear by beginning the report with a quote from President Reagan, who was then in office: "The American spirit . . . knows no ethnic, religious, social, political, regional or economic boundaries: the spirit that burned with zeal in the hearts of millions from every corner of the earth who came here in search of freedom." Yet the commission rejected appeals by ethnic and religious leaders and economists for a great expansion in the number of immigrants and in refugee admissions. The commission talked of immigration policy being out of control and mentioned the hardening of public attitudes, especially toward illegal immigrants. Above all, illegal entry had to be stopped or substantially slowed down; in Hesburgh's words, the commission recommended "closing the back door to undocumented/illegal migration," while opening the front door to legal immigrants a little wider. Immigration control was in the national interest as "the toleration of large-scale undocumented/illegal immigration can have pernicious effects on U.S. society."[52] Lawrence Fuchs, executive director for the commission, put the concerns of the commission thus:

> To say that immigrants and refugees will be admitted in substantial numbers [in an] open society does not mean limitless immigration. The application of both qualitative and quantitative limits is a function of national sovereignty. . . .
> . . . [the rule of the law demands that] the United States should not permit the buildup of an underclass society outside the protection of the law; and that measures to enforce the immigration law should be effective without themselves . . . promoting an abridgement of due process.[53]

The commission recommended a three-part program to "reduce the flow of undocumented/illegal migration." The recommendations called for increased border control and interior enforcement of immigration laws; the enactment of legislation to penalize employers for hiring illegal aliens; and a legalization program for illegal aliens present in the country from before January 1, 1980. Large-scale temporary-worker programs as a means to combating illegal entry were considered by the commission, but no recommendations were put forward.[54]

Congress responded by holding joint hearings in May 1981 under the chairmanship of Senator Alan Simpson and Representative Romano Mazzoli. Simpson and Mazzoli sought to build support on the basis of the employer sanctions and legalization package. Simpson, from Wyoming, and Mazzoli, from Kentucky, represented areas where immigration was not a major concern, so they had no interest groups from their constituencies tracking their activities.[55] Simpson and Mazzoli shared the concerns of the commission expressed by Fuchs, namely, the maintenance of the integrity and unity of the nation. Simpson wrote to the *Washington Post* of his warning against federal policies that "encourage the separation of groups of people because of language and cultural differences," adding that a "substantial proportion of these new persons and their descendants do not assimilate satisfactorily into our society. . . . Furthermore, if language and cultural separation rise above a certain level, the unity and political stability of our nation will—in time—be seriously eroded."[56] Mazzoli and Simpson were strongly supported by the White House, despite the opposition of certain factions from California and Texas that were active in the executive. Newspapers around the country also strongly supported the efforts of Simpson and Mazzoli.[57]

After extensive hearings, which allowed all groups to air their concerns, the Simpson-Mazzoli bill was introduced, with Mazzoli stating that the bill was "intended to bring immigration to the United States back under the control of the American people." In an attempt to satisfy all parties, they stressed the balance between ending illegal entry (through employer sanctions) and the generosity that was being shown to illegal aliens already resident in the United States. To appeal to business and agricultural interests, they updated and streamlined the existing H-2 temporary-worker program, so labor would still be available for the farms in the Southwest. The Senate version of the bill was unanimously approved. However the bill came to a halt in the House. The opposition of Hispanic and civil libertarian groups was reflected in the House debate. The Hispanic Caucus and Black Caucus criticized employer sanctions on the grounds that such sanctions would lead to discrimination against minority groups. Legalization of resident illegals was attacked by some congressmen as condoning lawbreaking. Growers attacked the modified H-2 program as too restrictive.[58]

Having failed in the 97th Congress, Simpson and Mazzoli tried again in the 98th Congress, in 1983. The Senate again passed the bill quickly. In the House, however, different amendments were proposed. Those sponsored by the Hispanic Caucus aimed at weakening employer sanctions and establishing a procedure for the filing of complaints arising from employer sanctions. An amendment designed to please agricultural interests proposed milder employer sanctions (this time to satisfy the employers) and a more generous temporary-worker program. Most amendments were defeated, including attempts to derail employer sanctions, but a broader temporary-worker program was accepted. The House finally passed the bill by a narrow vote. When the House-Senate conference met, after a number of delays, it deadlocked over employer sanctions, legalization, and temporary-worker programs.[59]

In the 99th Congress, in 1985, a streamlined bill was introduced. After seven days the bill was passed by the Senate. After much debate in the House, compromise was reached on the issue of agricultural labor, and in October 1986, the House passed the bill by a comfortable margin. President Reagan signed the Immigration Reform and Control Act into law in November 1986.[60]

Mazzoli wrote that IRCA represented "a delicate balance between widely divergent views and interests about immigration. The major challenge in shepherding the legislation through Congress was preserving the balance."[61] The act did indeed reflect the concerns of the major interest groups. On paper the act also reflected the intent of its architects, namely, to assert national control over the borders of the nation.

IRCA in its final form was characterized by four primary provisions:

1. Sanctions were established for employers who knowingly hired, recruited, or referred for a fee any alien who was not authorized to work in the United States. Workers had to be documented with, *inter alia*, a U.S. passport, birth certificate, social security card, driver's license, naturalization certificate, or a resident alien document. In a concession to Hispanic leaders and to employers, an article was added that stipulated that the sanctions would be terminated if the comptroller general determined that sanctions resulted in discrimination or unduly burdened employers, and if Congress jointly resolved to accept the comptroller's decision.

2. Discrimination based on national origin or citizenship was prohibited if the job applicant was a U.S. citizen or a legal alien who had filed

notice of intent to become a citizen. A special office was created within the Department of Justice to investigate and prosecute charges of discrimination.

3. Temporary resident status was provided for aliens who had resided in the country continuously since before January 1, 1982, and who were otherwise not excludable under immigration law. Such persons could receive permanent resident status after eighteen months if they could demonstrate a minimal knowledge of English and of U.S. history and government, or if they were pursuing study in those areas. Newly legalized aliens were barred from participating in most federally funded public assistance programs for five years.

4. The act established a seven-year special agricultural workers (SAW) program, which provided temporary resident status for aliens who had worked at least ninety days in agriculture in the United States during the year ending May 1, 1986. They could adjust to permanent resident status after one or two years, depending how long they had worked in U.S. seasonal agriculture. From 1990 through 1993, replenishment workers could be granted temporary resident status in the event of a shortage of agricultural workers. Replenishment workers who had worked at least ninety days a year for three years could receive permanent resident status.[62]

Thus checks and balances were instituted on the employer sanctions device to reassure the business and Hispanic groups, as well as others. Retroactive legalization was, in part, such a compromise, as were the special office in the Justice Department to fight discrimination that may arise from IRCA, the special agricultural program, and the promise that employer sanctions would be reevaluated if they caused discrimination or burdened employers. Subsequently, advocacy groups would win additional concessions through the courts. Such concessions were essential to shepherding IRCA through. However, such concessions had a fundamental influence on the federal government's ability to regulate and control transnational (illegal) migration. Limits were placed on the government's actions, resources were diverted from the actual stopping of undocumented migration to fulfill other IRCA requirements, and mechanisms were set up that, in effect, put IRCA in constant question (by empowering the comptroller general to, together with Congress, terminate employer sanctions).[63]

On the face of it, the physically most powerful country in the world should be able to seal its borders against illegal entry. The system of checks and balances, and the broader claims (compared with those in the past) interest groups could make on immigration issues, prevented this from happening. Drastic actions, such as mass deportation of undocumented aliens that occurred in the 1950s, were now beyond the pale of legitimate debate and politically untenable.

IMMIGRATION AND CITIZENSHIP: ASSESSING IRCA'S EFFECTS

In evaluating the significance of IRCA with regard to citizenship, we need to assess, first, the extent to which IRCA was successful in its stated goal of substantially reducing the entry of illegal aliens, and, second, the significance of IRCA's measures for the value of citizenship. IRCA is of interest in this regard in that illegal aliens were retroactively legalized. In each of these respects, the value of citizenship and the distinction between alien and citizen is brought into question.

By the end of the amnesty period for the legalization program (relating to legally authorized workers, or LAW), on May 4, 1988, and the end of the special agricultural workers program, on November 30, 1988, more than 3 million applications had been submitted for legal residence. Of those applications, more than 2.2 million had been filed by Mexican aliens. By mid-1990 almost all LAW applicants had been reviewed and 95 percent had been approved for temporary residence status. Of the one-half of the SAW candidates whose applications had been reviewed by that time, 93 percent had been approved for temporary residence. Temporary residence status was the first step; in the years 1989 to 1992 permanent resident status (the second step) was granted to 1.56 million formerly illegal aliens who had resided in the United States since at least 1982 and to 1.08 million aliens in the SAW program. Thus by the end of 1992 nearly all those eligible for permanent residence had attained it.[64]

Rules of eligibility were liberalized under pressure from the courts and advocacy groups.[65] Changes by the INS included greater flexibility on documentary proofs of eligibility for legalization and improved relations with agencies and groups helping immigrants.[66]

IRCA sought to curb, if not eliminate, the flow of illegal aliens into the country and reduce the number of illegal residents in the country. Adverse effects to be avoided were, in particular, an increase in discrimination against foreign-looking or -sounding persons, regardless of immigration status.[67] By mid-1989, IRCA was partially successful in its primary goals but reports from the General Accounting Office as well as private and state agencies indicated a pattern of discrimination against Hispanics following the enactment of IRCA, despite the strenuous legislative effort to avoid just this phenomenon.

Bean, Vernez, and Keely, of the Urban Institute-RAND Corporation research group, note the difficulty of assessing whether illegal immigration has changed since the inception of IRCA. The illegal population in the country has always been difficult to estimate, and there are different types of undocumented aliens, each of which may be affected differently by IRCA. Researchers have noted distinctions between "settlers," that is, immigrants who intend to settle in the United States, "sojourners," migrants who intend to return to their country of origin; and "commuters," persons who illegally cross the border on an almost daily basis to work. These distinctions bear on the number of illegal aliens in the country at a given time as distinct from the number of settlers. Similarly, the flow of illegal aliens across the border is larger than the number of aliens resident in the country (which accounts in part for the enormous number of annual apprehensions of undocumented aliens).[68]

IRCA has reduced the number of illegal settlers in the country by fiat of the legalization program. Has IRCA reduced the number of illegal entrants coming into the United States? Examination of apprehensions data is most useful for estimating the flow of illegal aliens (rather than the number of undocumented already in the country and staying put), especially for those crossing the Mexican border, where most illegal aliens enter the United States.[69]

Apprehensions data reflect the vicissitudes of actual illegal entries. Apprehensions increased, for example, from approximately 970,000 in fiscal year 1982 to 1,251,000 in fiscal year 1983, following the collapse of the Mexican economy. Since then, apprehensions have averaged more than 1 million a year, peaking at over 1,760,000 in fiscal year 1986. In fiscal years 1987 and 1988, apprehension figures declined to about 1,190,000 and 1,008,000 respectively. However, as White, Bean, and Espenshade note, apprehensions are affected by a number of factors, including some that are unrelated to IRCA, such as the Mexican economy, demographic changes in Mexico, or seasonal labor demands in the United States.[70]

Michael White and his coauthors estimated an overall decline in the number of apprehensions between November 1986 and September 1988 of close to 700,000 or about 35 percent less than would be expected in the absence of IRCA. About 12 percent of the decline was attributed to changes in border control efforts of the INS, 17 percent to the agricultural legalization effort, and the remaining 71 percent to what the researchers call the deterrent effect of IRCA.[71] Apprehensions for fiscal year 1989 were down about 20 percent from fiscal 1988, a positive sign for IRCA.[72]

The early, but limited, success of IRCA was followed by reports of an upswing in illegal migration. In fiscal year 1990, 1.16 million aliens were apprehended for attempting illegal entry, a significant increase from the previous year and a significant jump after a three-year decline. (In 1991 1.2 million, and in 1992 1.25 million, apprehensions were recorded.) A major reason for the increase was the proliferation of forged documents that allowed undocumented workers to get around IRCA requirements. The fact that employers are not required to verify the authenticity of the documents is in part a sign of how successful the advocacy groups were; pressure from such groups led the INS to institute more flexible rules on documentary proofs soon after the enactment of IRCA. By mid-1992 it had become evident that IRCA was not deterring, in any significant sense, the flow of undocumented aliens.[73]

Immigration, IRCA, and the Value of Citizenship

Writing before the enactment of the Simpson-Mazzoli bill, Peter Schuck noted that uncontrolled illegal immigration threatened the efficacy of the law, actually transformed aspects of classical immigration law, and, indeed, threatened to unravel traditional understandings of national community. New "social contracts," Schuck pointed out, were being negotiated every day between undocumented aliens and U.S. society, contracts that could not be nullified through invocations of sovereignty. Undocumented aliens raise children in the country (who attend local schools), join voluntary associations, and attend local churches. Changing political alliances and contemporary mores make, as the Hesburgh commission noted, the idea of mass deportation such as occurred in the 1950s beyond consideration. Transnational ties now become a basis for membership in American society.[74]

Thus the courts have been forced to accept the undocumented aliens, even prior to IRCA, as a fait accompli and to extend to these residents some form of legal recognition—simultaneously chipping away at concepts of consent, sovereignty, and self-determination. This was evident in the 1982 Supreme Court decision, *Plyler v. Doe*, which compelled a state to provide free public education to the children of undocumented aliens.

Such a decision inducted into the national community an undefined and indefinable group. More important, the decision eroded the concept of national sovereignty in that it conferred important benefits of membership in the nation as a result of social ties that have come into being between undocumented aliens and U.S. citizens. Thus the very ineffectiveness of the borders became the rationale for challenging their relevance to membership privileges.[75]

IRCA sought, of course, to confront this problem, to undermine the rationale that the overwhelming of the borders is a reason to, in effect, ignore them. However, in one respect, the authors of the act accept the position of the court in *Plyler*: retroactive legalization made potential members of undocumented aliens, because those persons have become part of the (national) community through day-to-day participation in that community. In practical terms, clearly, there was a limited degree of choice. In order to bring some control over the undocumented population, a large element of that population had to be legally recognized (the element longest in the country—long enough, presumably, to have "put down roots" in U.S. society). Legalization involves a trade-off: the sovereign prerogative to choose who enters the country is temporarily conceded in order to assert expected sovereignty in the future. Legalization poses its risks, as congressional critics pointed out. Above all, legalization may encourage others to enter the country illegally in the hopes of another amnesty at a later date. However, insofar as the drafters of the act had no option, the real test of IRCA was the law's efficacy in substantially diminishing the illegal alien population within the country and reducing significantly the flow of illegal entrants across the border. The wider significance of IRCA must be evaluated in the light of the general trends in immigration and citizenship that IRCA reflects and, possibly, reinforces.

If one assumes the economic and demographic pressures for undocumented immigration remain the same (or increase), it appears that the federal government will be unable to substantially reduce illegal immigration. The complex of interest groups, institutional relations, and normative changes in the area of immigration policy that has been described here inhibit full state control. Although the *principle* of "membership by proxy," of membership as a function of transnational connections, has not been recognized in IRCA, the ongoing flow of undocumented migrants forces some form of institutional recognition. Indeed, only four years after passage of IRCA, a special provision was added to the Immigration Act of 1990 for, in effect, the retroactive legalization of, primarily, undocumented Irish aliens.[76] Membership in the United States—indeed, U.S. citizenship—is not necessarily only a function of the civic tie to the state. (A further example of this phenomenon is the "family fairness" provision of the 1990 act: aliens legalized under IRCA could request immigrant visas for their family members. Spouses and children of legalized aliens in the United States before May 5, 1988, could not be deported either.)[77]

Furthermore, past history suggests that the naturalization rates of newly legalized aliens will be low due to a lack of interest on the part of resident aliens. Of the over 600,000 legal Mexican immigrants admitted from 1970 to 1979, only 16 percent had naturalized by the end of 1992. This is significant because Mexico is the largest source of legal immigrants. In addition, most illegal immigrants come from Mexico and they are likely to have a similarly low rate of naturalization.[78] Although immigrants from Asian countries have on average a higher propensity to naturalize, the readiness of immigrants from *all* regions to naturalize has diminished since 1965.[79] Aliens had benefited indirectly from the civil rights movement in the 1960s and from the effort to end discriminatory policies against aliens in areas like employment and schooling. More recently, aliens could also turn to state welfare support to an unprecedented degree. Thus, by the 1980s, the privileges of citizenship over and above that of resident alien status, primarily voting, holding public office, and serving jury duty, were not strong incentives to naturalize.[80]

(Making comparisons of naturalization rates with the earlier immigrations prior to the ending of ethnic quotas in 1965, especially with the immigration waves early this century, is problematic at best. As Reed Ueda writes, "A hierarchy of civil ranks—aliens ineligible for citizenship, territorial nationals, declarant for citizenship—proliferated. . . . Naturalization had been a casual and informal process [in the late nineteenth century and very early twentieth century], but gradually crude racist criteria and upgraded naturalization were applied to admit only 'suitable' aliens.")[81]

Lobbying hobbled IRCA both prior to and following its enactment. Special interest activity in this field is a relatively recent development. The ethnic and ideological criteria for immigration, which characterized American immigration legislation in the earlier decades of the twentieth century, are fading away. The formulation of criteria of entry into the United States poses a dilemma reflected in the deliberations of the Hesburgh commission. As the director of the commission, Lawrence Fuchs, put it, to address immigration policy the commission had to ask about fundamental issues of American identity, to ask "what kind of country are we?"[82] Fuchs notes that the Hesburgh commission was committed to upholding three principles: international cooperation, the United States as an open society, and the rule of the law. However, little was said as to how principles of "open society" and the "rule of the law" could be applied to immigration policy in practical terms. Such principles were wide enough for various parties to challenge the legitimacy of almost any immigration criterion and to demand that criteria under challenge be renegotiated.

How did this situation of being unable, in essence, to define the nation come about? Ethnic criteria, and concomitant ethnic divisiveness and competition in immigration issues go back to 1917. But more immediately, the elimination of ethnic criteria, paradoxically adding political strength to ethnic advocacy groups, was rooted in the 1965 immigration legislation. The effect of the 1965 law was to create a situation where no ethnic group, or even immigrants from any specific continent, were clearly dominant. This resulted in greater political "pull" for groups interested in promoting immigration of fellow ethnics, such as, for example, Soviet Jews, Irish, Poles, or refugees from Central America. The political effectiveness of such ethnic groups is particularly felt at the federal level, where Congress, which makes immigration policy, is susceptible to lobbying. State governments too can, and do, lobby for ethnic groups that are prominent within their jurisdictions.

Additional support for such ethnic lobbying comes from the underlying "Americanism" that has historically characterized this society, where a person is defined by his or her beliefs and not by his or her primordial identities. Consequently, less restrictive immigration policies are intellectually and politically supported by many liberal *and* conservative groups. Liberal groups, like the American Civil Liberties Union, certain Protestant churches, Catholic associations, and others support the free movement of people on humanitarian grounds. Conservative organizations and economists see an open immigration policy as a correlate of laissez-faire economics, a policy that would only be to the benefit of the American economy and society.[83] (Although California's Proposition 187 of 1994, which would strictly limit state educational and medical support for undocumented immigrants, was supported by most Republicans and conservatives, even there divisions became evident. Prominent conservatives like William Bennett and Jack Kemp, for example, opposed the proposition. Proposition 187 is discussed further in chap. 5.)

IRCA represents this "delicate balance of interests," a balancing act that limits the effectiveness of the law. These interests affected the drafting of the law and its subsequent implementation. INS regulations, on issues such as legalization, were liberalized as a result of court action by advocacy groups. The implementation of the law is under constant scrutiny and its efficacy under constant question.[84]

What about ideological criteria? Partly as a result of improvements in international relations, ideological criteria have been progressively watered down since security and political grounds for exclusion were encoded and enacted in the early 1950s. Take, for example, the provision that excludes aliens (immigrants and nonimmigrants) said to be subversive because of membership of certain political organizations (primarily Communist and anarchist groups) and aliens who advocate such "subversive" views.[85] This provision came under criticism during the Carter presidency in 1976 and 1977, primarily because it was believed to violate the Helsinki Accords reached in 1975 (the source of the Conference on Security and Cooperation in Europe, the CSCE). President Carter himself raised the issue in 1977 when he stated: "The Helsinki Agreement . . . insures that some . . . human rights shall be preserved. We are ourselves culpable in some ways for . . . restricting unnecessarily, in my opinion, visitation to this country by those who disagree with us politically." In addition the State Department came under fire for not seeking waivers for high-ranking Communist officials of Western non-Communist countries and for Communists wishing to address U.S. labor groups. In order to comply more fully with the Helsinki Accords' requirement that barriers on the free movement of people and ideas be reduced, the Foreign Relations Authorization Act passed in 1977 required the secretary of state to recommend that an alien excluded for belonging to a proscribed organization be admitted, unless it was determined that it was contrary to the security interests of the United States. More dramatically, the Moynihan-Frank Amendment of 1987 prohibited the exclusion or deportation of an alien "because of any past, current, or expected beliefs, statements, or associations which, if engaged in by a United States citizen . . . would be protected under the Constitution." The provision of the McCarran-Walters Act excluding Communist and anarchist groups has also been criticized for violating free speech rights under the First Amendment, but this has not been upheld by the courts. In this case the court recognized the traditional interpretation of the Constitution when it comes to foreign affairs.[86]

Other provisions of the security exclusions law have been criticized for giving foreign policy unjustified influence on exclusion decisions. However, the erosion of both foreign policy concerns and ideological distinctions in immigration matters is most graphically evident in the Refugee Act of 1980. Prior to 1980, statutes on refugees reflected ideological and foreign policy priorities and favored refugees from Communist countries. The Displaced Persons Act of 1948, for example, was to aid persons "fleeing Fascist or Soviet persecution." The Refugee Relief Act of 1953 was designed to "expedite the admission of refugees" from Communist countries. The Refugee Act of 1980 was enacted in order to arrive at a neutral and nonideological criterion for admitting refugees that would be consistent with the U.N. Protocol Relating to the Status of Refugees. A refugee is defined as an individual who has "a well-founded fear of being persecuted for reasons of race, religion, nationality, membership of a particular group or political opinion." However, the State Department had to provide an advisory opinion on all applicants. Critics complained that this partly undermined attempts to reach a neutral definition of refugee. The numbers of refugees admitted from the Soviet Union and Eastern Europe remained disproportionate from 1980 to 1988.[87] Organizational changes have been made, in response to such criticism, to minimize both the role of the State Department and ideological considerations.[88] Now the Immigration Act of 1990 has all but scrapped ideological tests in immigration matters.[89]

These developments—the ending of ethnic immigration categories and the weakening of ideological tests—are giving rise to universal or "neutral" and utilitarian definitions of who may and who may not enter the country. Neutral criteria, which have no ideological or ethnic bias, are a way of steering between the various parties interested in immigration policy. But neutral criteria also have a major impact on the nature of the state-society link.

Neutral and nondiscriminatory criteria are predicated on supranational or transnational authorities—organizations, institutions, and treaties— that transcend the state. This is evident, for example, in the Moynihan-Frank Amendment predication on the Helsinki Accords and the Refugee Act of 1980 grounded on the U.N. protocol on refugees. The state, in this case the federal government, is by definition a body with national and particular interests. Supranational authorities, in particular international human rights codes and institutions, provide a universal, transnational, and neutral reference for immigration policy. The distinction between citizen and alien is also eroded since, insofar as such supranational provisions are applied, *national* interests are less salient. It is interesting, in this context, that the Constitution ceases to end "at the water's edge" and is applied, at least by implication, to foreigners as well as to Americans. This is evident in the Moynihan-Frank Amendment.

Neutral criteria are also expressed another way, and that is in the form of utilitarian, economic measures for entry into the country. Although utilitarian categories have appeared since 1952, professionals, persons of "exceptional merit," and persons with required skills are for the first time now of central importance in the Immigration Act of 1990. The 1990 act set aside 140,000 visas for skilled and employment-related applicants in 1992, the first year the 1990 act took effect. (Just over 116,000 immigrants in fact came in 1992 in this employment-related category. This was a substantial increase over the previous year when about 59,000 employment-related immigrants were allowed in.) Others in this employment category include those who may receive immigrant visas if they invest at least $1 million (less in depressed rural areas) in new capital that will generate employment for at least ten Americans. Economic qualifications are neutral because no quality of an ideological (and certainly not an ethnic) character is inherent in an occupation or profession, or even in money.[90]

The developments leading up to, and following, the enactment of IRCA reveal the underlying processes that impinge on the value of citizenship: the economic disparities driving transnational migration, the ambiguity as to what defines an American citizen today, the competitive struggle of ethnic, business, and other groups to shape immigration policy in these equivocal circumstances, and, lastly, the institutional limitations of the American government in the face of these challenges. IRCA, in balancing these various interests, had the modest goal of attempting to assert simply "who is in charge" at the country's borders, a goal for which it strived with an initial degree of success. It is, however, the general failure of IRCA that marks a shift in the way membership is defined in American society.

The Recasting of Nationality

The concept of nationality was designed, in classic international law, to regulate relations among sovereign states. The individual had a legal status insofar as he or she was a member of a state, the object of international law. The individual's status was a function of membership in a state. States, as sovereign entities, decided fully who could become a national within their jurisdictional boundaries.[91] Indeed, the determination of who is a national was intrinsic to national self-determination. Citizenship, almost universally regarded as the domestic designation of nationality, was (and still is in many respects and in most countries) the cornerstone of the nation-state. With the devaluation of citizenship in the United States and in Western Europe, the concept of nationality is being recast from an expression of national self-determination to a legal device for protecting individual human rights. This has dramatic implications for state, society, and the international order.

Observers have pointed out the problematic nature of membership in the nation-state today (at least in the West) and have called for a reevaluation of how we conceive of state membership. Tomas Hammar has suggested using "denizen" to describe permanent residents without citizenship. Similarly, Rogers Brubaker talks of "dual membership" centered around citizenship, on the one hand, and "denizenship," on the other. He points out that access to rights is based primarily on residence, not on citizenship. The model of the nation-state where membership is "egalitarian, sacred, national, democratic, unique and socially consequential" is an anachronism. Yasemin Soysal puts forward a model for "postnational membership" where membership is based not on particularistic national criteria, but on a basis of "universal personhood." The rules regulating such membership are transnational and are rooted in the organization of the nation-state system itself.[92]

By formulating the changes that have taken place in the area of state membership in terms of the recasting of nationality, a specific *problematique* presents itself, one that leads to a number of fundamental questions about the emerging international order.[93] What is the basis of state legitimacy? What is the character of relations between state, society (NGOs and individuals), and the international legal system and institutions? What, in this new order, is the rationale behind borders and regulating cross-border flows? In the face of multiple state memberships, transnational ties, dual citizenships, and so on, how do we characterize the different kinds of ties between NGOs, individuals, and states?

These problems can be posed because the legitimacy of the state, in its classic nation-state form, is in question. The devaluation of citizenship, of the principles governing the relations of state and society, has, needless to say, widespread ramifications.

The state has lost control of international migration. The transnational ties that have developed, as a consequence, between the aliens and their associations and groups in the host society have had the effect of loosening state-society ties. A basic incompatibility has developed between private interests and the public interest, namely the national interest represented by the state. Thus, transnational ties cut across the vertical ties of the nation-state. This produces, Martin Heisler notes, three principle effects that erode the legitimacy of the nation-state.[94]

First, the ability of the state to govern comes into question. The regulatory failures in controlling transnational migration itself is the initial problem. Subsequently, the transnational ties that develop further constrain the autonomy of the state. Societal expectations of effective government are not met. The conflict between a number of states and the federal government over who should pay for the medical and other public costs of illegal immigrants is symptomatic of this issue in the U.S. case. (One may add, of course, other transnational activities, such as the globalization of industrial production. Corporations do not necessarily see their fortunes as a function of the national well-being of their "home" state. Jobs, technology, and resources will be exported abroad if it serves to enhance the profit margin.) Second, social and political conflicts arise out of the presence of foreign populations. Nationalist groups and those with interests that are threatened by foreign populations grow in strength. Extreme right-wing movements in Europe are obvious examples. Conversely, other elements have an interest in supporting the foreign population.

Third, and most important, the fundamental relationship between state and citizen is broken. Such a pact determines the basis of state authority and citizens' claims. It defines how resources should be distributed and how political power should be divided. It is a compact rooted in history, in which institutional and legal frameworks have been set. Above all, the pact is an expression of a community of character and of mutual aid. "The restraint of entry serves to defend the liberty and welfare, the politics and culture of a group of people committed to one another and to their common life."[95]

As Gary Freeman points out in the European case, the migrants have divided the working class into national and immigrant camps, reducing the power of the labor movement, undercutting support for general welfare benefits, and provoking a resurgence of nativist movements. In the United States, the withdrawal of communities into ethnic and racial "islands," a stress on "multiculturalism," and questions as to the political-cultural integrity of the country are increasingly prominent.[96]

Instead of the pact between state and citizen, we have a variety of links between the state and groups and individuals in its jurisdiction. Rights and privileges are a function of residency more than citizenship. The nature of links is varied: strong ties with citizens, somewhat less with a growing body of dual citizens, and even weaker ties with foreign residents.[97] Some residents and associations have transnational interests or organizational bases, making the connection weaker yet. The character of ties can differ. The connections of associations or individuals can be primarily economic (a transnational corporation or a seasonal worker) or political (such as those of transnational environmental movements). Membership of a nation, or of an ethnic group, is increasingly bifurcated from membership of a state.[98]

Clearly, the basis of (nation)-state legitimacy is eroding. The state, in the regions of concern here, turns to other sources to legitimate its actions. Populated by bodies of people it cannot absorb in the conventional sense, the state adopts international legal codes that can account for such transnational actors. Those actors themselves turn to such codes in making demands on the state. The character and role of state, society, and international institutions are, consequently, being transformed. Those codes, namely international human rights instruments, have become progressively more salient since, not coincidentally, the 1970s and the 1980s.

4

Western Europe and
the Age of Rights

The organizing principle of international relations has been, classically, the sovereign state. International law was a law for states, and states were the objects of that law. Individuals had a status in international law only insofar as they belonged to a state, and the individual's rights were a function of that person's nationality. Human rights, which in their present form were formulated in the aftermath of World War II, are primarily individual rights.[1] For this reason, human rights in the system of states were viewed in the ensuing two decades as, at best, an aspiration to be admired but not to be taken too seriously in the realpolitik of world politics. Similarly, the state's treatment of its own nationals was its sole concern.

Transnational migration, however, is contributing to changing the status of individuals and nongovernmental organizations in Western Europe and the United States, not just in theory but in practice as well. Transnational migration, we have noted, reached levels that were viewed as dangerously high in Western Europe and the United States in the 1970s and 1980s. The loss of state control compromised the distinction between "national" and "alien," a distinction central to the practice of sovereignty and national self-determination. Transnational migrants or any other transnational entities are by definition an anomalous element in a system of sovereign states. International human rights law up to that point had been of minor concern to states. However, in part under the impact of transnational migration, and in the wake of the failure of state attempts to control that migratory flow, international human rights have increasingly come to the fore. International human rights provide an institutional mechanism with which states are able to take account of these transnational elements. International human rights instruments are designed purportedly to protect "persons" as a transnational category and thus could fill a void that national laws, with their stress on nationality and national jurisdiction, could not fill. The status of individuals and nongovernmental organizations is, as a consequence, undergoing a dramatic change in international law, particularly in the area of human rights.

International human rights did not became significant because of any intrinsic normative concerns about human rights of the states involved, or due to the efforts of human rights organizations per se. Rather human rights codes became a mechanism through which states could respond to changing structural conditions and challenges.[2]

The analytic focus and objective of the following two chapters is to document the process of how states have turned to international human rights codes in the area of immigration. The shift by states to international human rights instruments was not intentional; rather, it was part of piecemeal strategy, having failed to bring such transnational migration under control, to deal with this challenge to state sovereignty. Through careful analysis and description one can observe the case-by-case reasoning that has led states to turn to international human rights instruments that were already in place but hitherto had been of little significance to states.

While the United States and Western European countries have all turned to international human rights instruments in accounting for these transnational actors, some have moved more quickly than others. The U.S. case is the most ambivalent in its move to international human rights instruments. This ambivalence is rooted in the more "elastic" political character of American national identity and institutions, which has resulted in the slower movement of the United States in this regard. Similarly, the French have been more hesitant than the Germans in turning to international human rights codes, particularly in accepting the right of individual petition on the basis of international human rights instruments.

In analyzing the movement to international human rights codes, the focus here will be on the judicial branch of the state. Although the state is made up of a number of institutional entities, all those entities are dependent on certain canons of legitimation, which are anchored in legal discourse. The courts do not wrest "the instruments of power" from other agencies of the state. The courts do, however, function to put into question claims of legitimacy that various agencies put forward for their authority. In this way, the courts have a critical role in constituting the state and in recentering the legal authority of the state.

The courts are also of special note in contemporary politics because there has been a massive increase in "judicial activism," which has constantly escalated in the past two to three decades. This is the case even in Western Europe where judicial and constitutional politics traditionally had a passive role. The newly salient role of the court brought civil and human rights to the fore and overcame continental etatism—that is, the belief that the prerogatives of the state, as embodied in the executive and legislative branches, supersede civil and human rights. In the traditional perspective, liberties were granted (and could be taken away) at the pleasure of the state itself. Conversely the legislatures have diminished in importance: they are involved less in *making* laws and more in debating what will survive the scrutiny of the third branch, the judiciary.[3]

Human Rights and State Sovereignty

Various legal instruments that promote human rights and make the individual an object of international law are evident as far back as the early twentieth century and include such documents as the Minorities Treaties of the League of Nations. The present covenants and conventions that purportedly guarantee human rights are derived from the Universal Declaration of Human Rights, which was adopted by the United Nations in 1948. Organizations or charters that have placed individual rights at the center, many based on the Universal Declaration, include the International Covenants on Civil and Political Rights and on Economic, Social, and Cultural Rights, the International Labor Organization, the European Convention on Human Rights, and the Inter-American System for the Protection of Human Rights. Doubts were, and are, expressed, however, whether these organizations and documents, which were derived from interstate agreements, have any prospect of being properly implemented. "It is more realistic," as R. J. Vincent puts it, "to render the attention that contemporary international law gives to the individual [and nonstate groups] as subsidiary themes to the law between states."[4]

The conceptual shift between the sovereign nation-state as the guiding principle to a rule of human rights in which the individual and his or her associations are the object of international law and institutions is a dramatic one indeed. A sovereign nation-state has borders and it has boundaries, which is to say there are sociological as well as political connotations to the state's territoriality. The borders enclose a *particular* concept of nationhood, of a mutual commitment to certain norms, institutions, and forms of political participation. Sovereignty is a means by which the imputed right to such (national) self-determination is guaranteed. The individual is identified by his or her membership in a political community, which is represented in, or embodied by, the state.

Human rights, on the other hand, are *universal*. Every human being in every society is a carrier of such rights. They do not change with geography, culture, or stage of development, and they do not distinguish between race, class, sex, religion, or national origins. Human rights are not an abstract good but positive rights as defined in international codes or instruments such as the Universal Declaration. Human rights include "immunities"—freedom from torture, for example—and affirmative rights, such as freedom of speech and assembly. No comprehensive political theory on the relationship of the individual vis-à-vis the state is posited in international human rights codes. The idea of rights, however, imply political and moral principles.[5] Through the stress on universal and transnational rights, for example, distinctions between "national" and "alien" are at least in question—distinctions that are critical to the nation-state and the principle of national self-determination.

Human rights, however, must have a reasonable chance of being met if they are to have some significance. Herein we enter the area of implementation. Individuals and their organizations must have the means to make claims on the state in terms of such transnational rights, that is, in terms of international human rights codes. Institutional avenues and procedures have to be developed to facilitate individual claims in terms of such codes.[6] This operational question is addressed in this and the next chapter. To what extent *can* the individual and nonstate groups make claims on the state, in the United States and in the Western Europe, in terms of international human rights codes?

If one can establish that such claims can be made, then a transformation is taking place in the very structure of international society. The state's legitimacy, among other things, is then rooted less in popular sovereignty and national self-determination and more in transnational human rights. The state then does not dictate its jurisdictional scope so much as its legal and political procedure situates the state in the international order. The state's role, and the relationship between the state and its nationals, is then increasingly defined by the international order, specifically by international human rights codes and institutions. Thus, human rights act as "a kind of midwife" for the transformation of international politics.[7]

International Human Rights Instruments

Tens of documents of the United Nations and other international or regional institutions are considered international human rights instruments. Certain major codes, however, serve as the foundation of international human rights law, and those instruments are the chief focus of concern in this study.

The U.N. Charter declared that the United Nations would promote universal respect for human rights. The charter, an international treaty to which nearly all states have subscribed, dealt with human rights in vague, inoperational terms, with the exception of a nondiscrimination clause vis-à-vis race, sex, language, or religion. The charter internationalized human rights, however, and, legally speaking, took human rights out of the area of domestic jurisdiction.

In 1948, the U.N. General Assembly adopted the Universal Declaration of Human Rights, which became the basic statement on human rights and the trunk from which other human rights instruments grew. The rights under the declaration included security of person, freedom from slavery, freedom from arbitrary arrest or interference in private life, freedom of association, religion, and opinion, right to choose a form of education, right to marry, and right to own property. The Universal Declaration is not an international treaty and, as such, it does not have the legally binding character of treaties. It is a declaration, not an agreement to be signed and ratified. But many view the declaration, given the repeated reference to it, to have the status of customary international law—that is, an international and general practice that is accepted and observed as law.[8]

The International Covenant on Civil and Political Rights and the International Covenant on Economic, Social, and Cultural Rights legislated what the Universal Declaration aspired to. Both the covenants were opened for ratification in 1966. It took another ten years before the thirty-five states ratified the covenants, the number required to bring the covenants into legal force. In 1976, a Protocol to the Covenant on Civil and Political Rights that enables private parties to file complaints to the U.N. Human Rights Committee (if a state that has ratified the protocol is involved) was opened for ratification.

The International Covenant on Civil and Political Rights requires states to ensure rights to life, due process of law, freedom of expression and religion, freedom to travel, cultural rights of minorities, participation in government, equality and protection from discrimination, and the right to marry and have a family. Most rights, including freedom of association, movement, and expression, can be curtailed in "time of public emergency which threatens the life of the nation." Some rights are subject to derogation for public order, health, or morals.

The International Covenant on Economic, Social, and Cultural Rights concerns work conditions, social security, housing and living standards, and other issues. Here, the state is not required to give immediate effect to these rights but merely to "take steps" to the extent its resources allow to realize these rights.

Other U.N. human rights treaties include the Convention on the Prevention and Punishment of Genocide (1948), the International Convention on the Elimination of All Forms of Racial Discrimination (1965), Convention on the Political Rights of Women (1981), and the Convention against Torture and Other Cruel, Subhuman, or Degrading Treatment (1987). States are bound by these human rights instruments only if they have ratified them, unless, through repeated use or reference, an instrument has taken on the status of international customary law, which is legally binding on all states.

The European Convention on Human Rights was established by the member states of the Council of Europe to realize the goals of the Universal Declaration of Human Rights. Indeed, the convention, which was adopted in Rome on November 4, 1950, by and large incorporated the human rights as proclaimed in the Universal Declaration.

The inter-American system for the protection of human rights has two distinct legal sources: the Charter of the Organization of American States (OAS), and the American Convention on Human Rights. The Inter-American Commission on Human Rights is an organ based on both instruments. The American Convention on Human Rights was adopted in 1969 and entered into force in 1978 after eleven states ratified it. The United States has signed the document but the Senate has yet to ratify it. The American convention is patterned on the European convention but also draws on the American Declaration of the Rights and Duties of Man of 1948 and the International Covenant on Civil and Political Rights.

A member state of the OAS, such as the United States, that has not ratified the American convention is subject to the human rights elements that have its constitutional basis in the OAS Charter. Until 1970, the human rights regime of the OAS was weak and uncertain. Then the Protocol of Buenos Aires, which was drafted in 1967, entered into force. The newly revised charter put human rights at the center of its concerns by recognizing the American Declaration of the Rights and Duties of Man as a standard for judging the human rights compliance of all OAS member states.[9]

The Conference on Security and Cooperation in Europe (CSCE) was established by the Helsinki Final Act, in 1975, by the Soviet Union, the United States, Canada, and thirty-two European countries. The CSCE's name was changed to the Organization for Security and Cooperation in Europe (OSCE) at the Budapest meeting in December 1994. The organization's name was changed in order to raise its international profile. With the collapse of Soviet communism, membership of the now OSCE is expanding quickly. By the end of 1994 it had fifty-three members. The role of the organization is also being transformed. At first designed to encourage peaceful coexistence between the East and West blocs, it is now an intergovernmental institution for the promotion of human rights. The OSCE has had, and will continue to have, follow-up conferences that review compliance of the OSCE by participating states, and to revise and amplify the instrument. The rights promoted by the OSCE include freedom of thought and belief, freedom to travel, and freedom from discrimination on racial, ethnic, or religious grounds (see chap. 6).

What is clear about many of the international human rights codes, particularly those that were formulated in the early postwar period, is that the *state* is still realistically recognized as the subject of international relations. It was almost always up to a state, and not private parties, for example, to lodge complaints to the United Nations or to the regional organs about human rights violations. Even then, until two decades ago, these instruments were of little political and sociological consequence. International migration and the impact of that migration is one important factor behind two interrelated developments that became clear by the 1970s and 1980s. Individuals and other private parties were increasingly able to petition governments on the basis of international human rights codes (or regional instruments derived from international codes), and these instruments, whose source is interstate agreements, became autonomous or semiautonomous of the states themselves.

The impact of international human rights law in this period is striking in Western Europe. In the United States, by contrast, the impact is equivocal; yet even there the approach to international human rights law took a distinctly positive turn in the late 1970s, a turn that is likely to become more pronounced.

The European Convention on Human Rights

Whatever ambivalence the American courts have had about the increasing significance of international human rights law in recent years, the Europeans, in contrast, have demonstrated little reticence. The European Convention on Human Rights (ECHR) has acquired the status of a "constitutional instrument of European public order in the field of human rights."[10] The ECHR, which was signed in November 1950, originally stressed the role of states. It also, in its first twenty-five years of operation, generated few cases. Since the 1970s individual claims through the institutions of the ECHR have been greatly facilitated. The case load of ECHR organs has also skyrocketed in this period. Not coincidentally, this occurred at the time when the permanent presence of foreign populations was recognized; aliens have been a driving force behind the increased salience of ECHR codes and institutions. The convention was originally signed by twelve states. By January 31, 1995, it had been ratified by thirty-four states, with the promise of still more members; with the collapse of the Soviet Union and the breakup of Czechoslovakia and Yugoslavia, the territorial reach of the convention has been moving progressively to the east.

The ECHR is not one of the treaties establishing the European Union, even though the preamble of the convention states that the aim of the Council of Europe, the parent body of the ECHR, is "the achievement of greater unity between its Members." The ECHR institutions, the Commission of Human Rights and the Court of Human Rights, are quite distinct from the EU's Court of Justice, which interprets and applies community law. However, the convention secures the "harmonization" of the laws of contracting states; new legislation and constitutional provisions need to comply with the convention and old laws need to be amended accordingly, bringing the legal practice of member states more closely in line. Furthermore, all the members of the European Union have ratified the convention and the EU's Court of Justice has determined that the convention forms part of Community Law. Hence, the convention is the nucleus of a European constitution and a European Bill of Rights.[11]

The European Convention on Human Rights, on the other hand, is not simply a regional institution that reflects purely regional concerns. The convention, in content and aspiration, is the realization of international human rights in Europe. The convention is both "inward looking and outward looking," as a body of procedural and substantive law for the European arena, and as a part of "the wider fabric of international efforts for the promotion of human rights."[12]

The Statute of the Council of Europe, which was signed in May 1949, made human rights not only an objective of the council but a condition of membership. Two motives were apparent. First, it was a reaction to Nazism, at the hands of which many of the leading statesmen of the period had personally suffered. Second, democratic Europe was establishing its ideological grounding in the conflict with the Communist bloc. "The present struggle is one which is largely being fought in the minds and consciences of mankind," remarked Sean MacBride, the Irish foreign minister, at the signing of the convention in 1950.[13] Western Europe would carry the flag of universal human rights and freedoms. When the Council of Europe began work on drafting the ECHR in 1949, it had at hand a statement of such rights in the United Nation's Universal Declaration.[14] Thus, the founding of the convention contained the seed of individual rights and the promise that individuals would be the subject of international institutions, but the convention was also born in the first flush of the *interstate* struggle between the Western alliance and the Communist bloc. Initially, the state dimension came to dominate in the ECHR and its institutions.

Rights in the convention drawn from the Universal Declaration include the right to life, liberty, and the security of person; protection from torture, inhuman or degrading treatment or punishment; fair and public hearings in criminal proceedings; respect for private and family life; freedom of thought, conscience, and religion; freedom of expression; freedom of peaceful assembly and of association; freedom to marry and have a family; freedom of parents to choose the kind of education to be given to their children; and freedom from arbitrary arrest, detention, or exile, among other rights.

The convention is universal in that in form and content it is largely drawn from the Universal Declaration; it expressly aims to advance international human rights in Europe; anyone, whether a national of a contracting state or not, can make claims under the convention; and the judges on the Court of Human Rights do not have to be members of any contracting state.[15] The ECHR has been cited in U.S. courts as an instrument of international human rights law.

International law is not only part of the legal background of the convention but different articles refer explicitly to international law. Such international legal obligations, consequently, need to be expressly taken into account under the convention. For example, under Article 7(1) it is held that, "No one shall be held guilty of any criminal offense . . . which did not constitute a criminal offense under national or international law." Article 15(1) reads that, "In time of war or other public emergency . . . any High Contracting Party may take measures derogating from its obligations under the Convention . . . provided that such measures are not inconsistent with its other obligations under international law." Article 26 states that a case is admissible only after all domestic remedies have been exhausted "according to the generally recognized rules of international law." Under Article 1 of Protocol No. 1 no person may be deprived of his possessions subject to, inter alia, "the general principles of international law." Other international treaties are also used for interpretive purposes when the convention omits rights guaranteed in other international instruments, when another instrument can amplify on the convention, or when a convention provision is itself derived from another international treaty.[16]

However, there is a regional dimension to the ECHR as well. The convention in certain cases alters the rights delineated in the Universal Declaration. The convention, for example, omits the provision of the Universal Declaration that no one may be compelled to belong to an association. This omission accommodates the "closed-shop" trade unions active in some European countries. The Universal Declaration provision to secure freedom of movement did not appear in the original convention document but was added as part of Protocol No. 4 in 1963. Most notably, the convention limits itself to civil rights. The list of economic and social rights in the Universal Declaration does not appear at all. The European democracies in 1950 regarded (and, needless to say, still regard) economic and social standards as at best "aspirational" and not rights as such. Furthermore, such rights as the right to work or housing would abridge individual liberties.[17] This, after all, was what was at the root of the ideological struggles with the Communist bloc.

The coloring that international human rights documents take, like the ECHR, as a result of interstate conflicts is significant. Even though these instruments later take on a status as institutions that are autonomous or semiautonomous of states, the specific states that had a pivotal role in designing these instruments have a hand in shaping the emerging international order, even as they fade into the background in military, economic, and political terms and as sovereign, even "hegemonic," entities.

ALIENS AND NATIONALS

As in the case of other international human rights instruments, distinctions between aliens and nationals or citizens are not specifically prohibited in the ECHR. As in other international human rights instruments, however, the convention bestows rights on "persons," and not on citizens per se. Indeed, the convention explicitly states that the enjoyment of rights and freedoms set forth in the convention shall be secured without discrimination on the basis of, inter alia, national origin or association with a minority. Differential treatment between aliens and nationals is allowed where it is explicitly provided for. Thus, Article 16 of the convention provides for restrictions on the political activity of aliens. (In Protocols to the Convention that were signed in 1963, Protocol No. 4, and 1984, Protocol No. 7, aliens as aliens are given certain protections.) Conversely, no one can be deprived of the right to enter the territory of the state of which he or she is a national (citizen).

The convention does not guarantee aliens the right to enter and reside in a country, as such.[18] If this were the case, how can transnational migrants and aliens make claims on a contracting state in terms of the ECHR? Discrimination on the basis of alienage, which prevents the entry or residence of an alien in a country, violates the convention if the discrimination interferes with other protected rights. Thus, aliens can make claims on citizenship and immigration laws on the basis of Article 3 (inhuman or degrading treatment), Article 5 (liberty of person), Article 6 (fair and public hearing), Article 8 (respect for private and family life), and Article 12 (right to marry). Such claims are also made in conjunction with Article 14 (nondiscrimination on the basis of national origin). Aliens can make claims through the ECHR institutions if a contracting state is a concerned party. Resident aliens can, of course, draw on almost the full gamut of articles in the convention.[19]

The ability of aliens to make claims on states, in terms of the ECHR, plays a significant role in changing the character of the state and its basis of legitimacy. Alien claims were also significant in helping to bring the ECHR to the center stage of European political and social life in the late 1970s.

THE MACHINERY: FROM STATE PRACTICE TO TRANSNATIONAL NORMS

Two institutions were established by the convention: the Commission of Human Rights and the Court of Human Rights. Supervisory functions on the enforcement of rights are also conferred on the Committee of Ministers of the Council of Europe.

The commission has the number of members equal to the number of states that have ratified the ECHR. They are elected by the Committee of Ministers. The number of Court of Human Rights judges equals the number of members of the Council of Europe. They are elected by the Parliamentary Assembly of the Council of Europe. Commission members, as well as the judges, do not have to be nationals of member states. Indeed, a Canadian has served on the Court of Human Rights.

By ratifying the convention, a state accepts the jurisdiction of the commission to receive complaints from other state parties. Very few interstate petitions have been filed, apparently in order not to disturb diplomatic ties. The right of an individual to file a complaint with the commission is dependent on that state specifically recognizing the right of individual petition. Article 25 of the convention states that the commission may receive petitions from any person, nongovernmental organization, or group of persons provided that the state that is the object of the petition recognizes that right (by ratifying, separately from the ECHR as a whole, Article 25). Nearly all the state parties have ratified Article 25. France, for example, ratified the convention in 1950 but ratified Article 25 only in 1981.[20]

The commission determines the admissibility of a petition.[21] Petitions that are incompatible with the convention's provisions, "manifestly ill-founded," or are an "abuse of the right of petition" are rejected. Part of this process of admissibility is determining whether domestic channels for resolving any dispute have been exhausted. Only a small percentage of cases reaches the postadmissibility stage of proceedings. The commission lacks the formal power to adjudicate a case; only the Committee of Ministers or the court can do that. If the commission fails to reach a friendly settlement it draws up a report on the case. The report is transmitted to Committee of Ministers, with the decision whether the case should be referred to court left up to the commission. In recent years, the commission has referred an increasing proportion of the cases to the court. This is very significant because the Committee of Ministers, which decides cases that are not referred to the court, is constituted such that national and state interests take priority rather than transnational human rights per se. The committee, which is staffed by foreign ministers, was instituted when the convention was drafted with an eye to winning over as many states as possible to ratify the ECHR.[22] Its fading importance in recent years is only one sign of the shift from a focus on state practice to a focus on individuals and NGOs and of the autonomy of international codes and institutions like the ECHR.

The Court of Human Rights jurisdiction includes cases referred to it by the commission or a state party. No state has espoused the case of one of its nationals before the court. However, individual petitions have gained increased importance since the 1970s and 1980s. A 1970 ruling allowed the commission to designate a counsel for nonstate applicants before the court. Then, in 1983, revised rules of the court gave individual applicants the right to participate and be represented in proceedings before the court. Thus, individuals and NGOs now have a standing before the court that is similar to that of the commission or state parties, even though individual claims cannot be made directly to the court. Indeed, Protocol No. 9, which was only recently opened for signature on November 6, 1990, formalizes the status of the individual vis-à-vis the court and, moreover, places him or her almost on par with state parties. The Protocol No. 9 states that "persons, non-governmental organizations or groups of individuals," as well as state parties and the commission, can, having submitted a petition to the commission, directly bring a case before the court. Protocol No. 9 entered into force on October 1, 1994. The protocol had by that point been ratified by fifteen member states, including Germany (but not yet by France). Most of the remaining members, it appears, are likely to ratify the protocol as well.

Adding to the trend away from focusing on state practice and toward stressing individual rights are the voting patterns of the judges on the court. In the International Court of Justice, it is very rare for a judge to vote against the position of his or her own government in disputes before the court. This practice, however, is very frequent in the European Court of Human Rights. In more than half of the judgments, judges voted against their own governments, most frequently in unanimous judgments. Even when the minority votes in favor of a government, however, the national judge sometimes votes with the majority against his own government. This pattern has become even more accentuated since the late 1970s.[23] This is all the more significant as the Court of Human Rights has become the chief interpreter of the convention's provisions.

Although the discussion here emphasizes the international and regional dimensions of the ECHR, the convention influence is further felt in the countries that have incorporated the substantive provisions of the code into their domestic law. (Those countries include Germany, France, the Netherlands, Spain, Switzerland, and Turkey.) For these countries, judgments by the European Court of Human Rights have a direct effect on domestic courts. Domestic courts in such cases are compelled to follow the convention and the case law emerging from Strasbourg closely. The municipal courts thus play a vital role as it is mostly before these courts that the convention's provisions are invoked.[24]

This development, of domestic courts following the rulings of Strasbourg and of the provisions of the convention more generally, has moved forward dramatically since the early 1980s. Domestic courts have abandoned any reservations they had as an ever increasing case law becomes available from Strasbourg. The traditionally autonomous approach of the French judiciary softened with a 1980 decision that gave an international treaty (including the convention) priority over a municipal law enacted after the treaty had taken effect. In Germany, a 1987 decision dramatically increased the authority of the convention, when the Federal Constitutional Court held that the basic law of the German Constitution, formally having the status of ordinary law, had to be interpreted in the framework of the ECHR. Furthermore, legislation has been enacted in Germany in order to comply with, or avoid adverse findings of, the European court. With the unification of Germany, the convention also became applicable to what was East Germany.[25]

In countries where the ECHR is recognized as international law, but is not yet incorporated domestically (including Denmark, Sweden, the United Kingdom, Iceland, Ireland, and Norway), case law coming out of Strasbourg does not directly affect legal proceedings in their national courts. Residents of these countries can appeal directly to the European commission but getting a hearing before the European court is a much more difficult and time-consuming process than it would be before national courts. Still, even those countries, particularly Britain, have increasingly had to take account of the ECHR and pass legislation to preempt unfavorable rulings.[26] Interestingly, litigation of a British origin takes up a disproportionate part of the case load of the European Court of Human Rights.[27]

TRANSNATIONAL MIGRATION AND THE EUROPEAN CONVENTION ON HUMAN RIGHTS

The changes from the 1970s and the 1980s that have brought the convention to the fore and have indicated a shift in the object of international law and institutions, from that of states to that of individuals and NGOs, have been nothing short of breathtaking. In addition to the structural changes mentioned already—an increasing number of cases referred to the European court instead of the Council of Ministers, the much greater access of the court to individuals, the independence of the court vis-à-vis the state parties, the dominant role of the court in interpreting the ECHR and indeed in forming a European constitutional jurisprudence based on international human rights, and the increasing accountability of national courts to Strasbourg—other developments have occurred in this period.

States, quicker to waive objections to admissibility and accept that cases should be treated on their merits, have been increasingly ready to introduce legislation and modify administrative practice if necessary.[28] The result is that more applications are declared admissible. Not only were more cases decided by the court, but the court found an increasing proportion of the cases as violations and awarded greater numbers of reparations. In some respects, the rate of these changes was not linear but almost geometric.[29]

Pushing this process along are, in this same period, individual nonstate applications to the European commission. (State applications have been rare, illustrating the limited use of interstate petitions as a mechanism for upholding human rights.) The number of registered applications jumped dramatically in the 1970s (by about 100 percent from the mid-1960s) and, though stricter rules were instituted on what applications could be registered, which resulted in a slight dip, applications returned to high levels in the 1980s.[30]

As only a small, if increasing, percentage of the cases reach the court in Strasbourg, more significant is the increasing case load of the court. In the first eighteen years of the court's existence, from 1959 to 1976, the court decided only 17 cases and in only 7 cases was at least one provision of the convention found to have been violated. During the seven-year period between 1978 and 1984 (no cases were decided in 1977), the court reached a decision on 50 cases and found at least one violation in 39 cases. Comparing the two periods, we find an average of only one case per year in the first period and nearly triple that number in the second period. Whereas in 41 percent of the cases a violation was found in the first period, the same is true for 78 percent of the cases in the second period. The case load has continued to grow, with decisions being made on 141 cases from 1985 to 1990. From 1991 to 1993 decisions were made on 213 cases, though that number was inflated to some extent by a series of judgments on the same issue.[31]

The timing, the years in which all these changes occurred, is clearly significant. Transnational migration has a notable role in challenging sociolegal and political assumptions about citizenship. The nation-state framework cannot continually absorb what are, legally speaking, anomalous actors—actors who "don't belong" but whom the state is unable to expel. International human rights, with its premise of universal "personhood," becomes an alternative framework for aliens, for states, and, consequently, for the states' nationals as well.

The linkage between transnational migration and the increased importance of the convention is not simply temporal but is substantive as well. Aliens are one force (though not the only force) behind the massive increase of cases coming before, and claims made on the basis of, the ECHR. The states' concessions to the convention and its institutions are also indicative of a recognition of a changing international landscape. From 1976 to 1983, about one-quarter, on average, of the applications registered by the Commission of Human Rights were lodged by aliens.[32] Furthermore, these figures do not include applications lodged by nationals in cases involving aliens such as, for example, family reunification cases. This is a formidable number, well out of proportion to the size of the foreign populations in European countries.[33] The significance of transnational migration for the now central role of the convention is also evident in major cases that have come before the Commission and the Court of Human Rights.

RESHAPING THE STATE: NATIONALITY AND INTERNATIONAL LAW

> Whereas under general international law a State has the right, in virtue of its sovereignty, to control the entry and exit of foreigners into and out of its territory; and whereas it is true that a right or a freedom to enter the

territory of States, Members of the Council of Europe, is not, as such, included among the rights and freedoms guaranteed in . . . the Convention; whereas, however, a State which signs and ratifies the [Convention] must be understood as agreeing to restrict the free exercise of its rights under general international law, including its right to control the entry and exit of foreigners, to the extent and within the limits of the obligations which it has accepted under that Convention . . .[34]

The ECHR does not recognize a right to nationality per se and, as the preceeding quotation illustrates, the commission has ruled that aliens do not have a right in and of itself to enter a member country. But in restricting the border control of states on the basis of universal (not national) criteria, and in recognizing the rights of aliens on the basis of an attachment they may have to a territory (through marriage, for example), and not on the basis of citizenship, national-ethnic background, or ideological beliefs, the convention recognizes, in effect, a right to nationality as a human right.[35] The state is thus in the process of being turned on its head; instead of acting as a sovereign body that represents and embodies a nation, it is now accountable to international rules and institutions for the treatment of people in its jurisdiction. The concept of nationality is recast internationally as well as domestically—the two levels are obviously interlinked.

Important cases and legal interpretations of the convention that illustrate the recasting of nationality, under the convention, can be briefly noted. In a major case, the East African Asians case, a charge was made that the United Kingdom's Commonwealth Immigrants Act of 1968 violated Article 3, namely, that "no one shall be subject to . . . inhuman or degrading treatment." The act had been hastily passed in reaction to an influx of citizens of the United Kingdom and Commonwealth countries of Asian origin who left East Africa because of discriminatory policies there. The 1968 act held that only those whose parents or grandparents had been born in the United Kingdom could relocate to Britain. The commission found that Article 3 had been violated.

The East African Asians had suffered degrading treatment because of, in substance if not in form, their race. (This decision was reached independently of Article 14, which prohibits discrimination on the basis of national origin.) Many of the East African Asians had nowhere else to go. Immigrant legislation thus discriminates on grounds of race, according to the convention, if that legislation results in "inhuman" or degrading treatment. The group singled out in such a manner does not have to be, necessarily, citizens of the state concerned for Article 3 to be violated.[36]

The clause in Article 8, that everyone has the right to respect for his or her family life, has proved a particularly useful basis to establish an attachment of aliens to a country. Family life may be threatened when the state determines that the acts of one member conflict with its "interests." The commission conversely is concerned that a bona fide family relationship exists (in terms of cohabitation, for example; stepchildren, illegitimate children, or polygamous unions are not ipso facto considered outside the family unit), and if the family could unite in another country other than a respondent state in a given case. Article 8 is often the basis of claims in conjunction with Article 14 (freedom from discrimination). For example, the Court of Human Rights in 1985 ruled a U.K. law that allowed a foreign wife to join her husband legally settled in the United Kingdom, but refused foreign husbands the right to join their lawfully resident wives, is a violation of Article 8, in conjunction with Article 14, because of the patent sexual discrimination. The British government subsequently amended the immigration law to take account of this ruling.[37]

The Fourth Protocol of the European Convention, which entered into force in 1968 (and still remains to be ratified by a number of states) added protections for aliens and for nationals, classically understood. Article 2 of Protocol No. 4 states that "*Everyone* lawfully within the territory of a State" shall have freedom of movement within that state (emphasis added). The protocol also prohibits collective expulsion of aliens. On the other hand, Protocol No. 4 adds explicit protections for nationals, in the traditional sense, which, of course, reinforces distinctions between aliens and citizens; the protocol states that a national may not be expelled from, or denied entry to, his or her state. These clauses overcame a prior ruling of the commission that, "the right of an individual to reside within the territory of his own State is not as such guaranteed under any of the provisions of the Convention." However, special provisions for citizens are an exception that proves the rule; only one other article favors citizens, namely Article 16, which authorizes restrictions on aliens' political activity. Differential treatment against aliens cannot be read into the convention by implication. Where discrimination against aliens is permissible, it is, in those exceptional circumstances, explicitly noted. (Indeed, Protocol No. 1, which partly concerns property rights, has been interpreted as favoring aliens over citizens.)[38]

THE EUROPEAN UNION AND IMMIGRATION

Immigration only became a major issue area in the European Community, now the European Union, by the 1980s and 1990s. The European Union was historically never designed to handle the *transnational* movement of people. The Treaty of Rome of 1957 that created the European Economic Council (EEC) provided for the free movement of persons on a purely regional basis—persons from non-EU countries were excluded from this provision.[39] Furthermore, the EU's initial purpose was economic integration. Until recently, it was never concerned with the "rights" of citizens or residents in member countries unless they directly concerned the issues of workers and their movement inside the community. The problem of socially or politically integrating or excluding foreigners was outside the mandate of the European Union. Finally, and perhaps most important, there has always been a tension, and an ambiguity, between the EU's status as a supranational organization and its role as an interstate organization that simply reflects the combined interests of its members.[40] The Council of Europe, focused on political, civil, social, and cultural issues on the one hand, and rooted in truly international instruments (such as the Universal Declaration of Human Rights) on the other, was much better situated to "assimilate" transnational activities such as migration.[41]

The European Union began to take the immigration issue much more seriously when its mandate extended beyond the strictly economic; the supranational dimension came to be perceived, at least, as more salient; and the numbers of foreigners in Europe, including the massive onrush of asylum seekers and immigrants from Eastern Europe, became too large to ignore. It was only *after* Western Europeans realized that the guest workers had become permanent residents and that national governments had decided to stop recruiting foreign labor that ministers in 1974 identified migrant labor as a key factor of social policy at the community level. (The accession of three new member states, Denmark, Ireland, and the United Kingdom, and recessionary pressures were also an impetus to bring migrant issues to the forefront of community concerns.) Prior to 1974 immigration issues were considered the exclusive preserve of the sovereign state. By 1976 the Council of Ministers advocated a community approach to the nationals of third countries.[42]

Only by the mid-1980s, however, did the union begin to outline what was meant by a common approach to the migrant issue. In 1985 the commission of the European Union took a "decision" that introduced a procedure "for prior communication and consultation on migration policies in relation to non-member countries." The European Court of Justice annulled the decision but gave full recognition of the need for harmonization of policy toward foreigners.

The Single European Act agreement reached in 1985 and entered into force in 1987 (and the first major amendment to the Treaty of Rome) sought, inter alia, an "internal market . . . without internal frontiers." To facilitate such free movement of persons, the member states had to affirm that they "shall cooperate, without prejudice to the powers of the Community, in particular as regards the entry, movement and residence of nationals of third countries." Nevertheless, sovereignty issues are still a sticking point: "Nothing in these provisions shall affect the right of Member States to take such measures as they consider necessary for the purpose of controlling immigration from third countries."[43]

The Schengen agreement of 1985 between Germany, France, and the Benelux countries also sought the elimination of common border controls by 1990. By the end of 1993, however, the agreement was yet to be implemented or even ratified by all the relevant legislatures. This agreement was viewed as a "test" for technical solutions to removing controls throughout the community. With the Maastricht Treaty in 1991, a commitment was made to the "formal and actual harmonization" on asylum policies, immigration, and aliens' status by 1996.

The reasoning of the EU institutions, notes Giuseppe Callovi, was (and is) clear: to loosen internal border controls, they had to compensate by strengthening the community's external borders. At the same time, the member states could not overcome the sovereignty issue built into EU decision making. Thus there were repeated references to the "right of Member States to take such measures that they consider necessary for the purpose of controlling immigration from third countries." Nevertheless, it also became apparent that external border controls did not imply "fortress Europe" because there was a strong commitment to human rights, particularly in the area of family reunification and political asylum.[44] (On what other substantive basis, one can ask parenthetically, could such a EU-wide policy be based? Ideology? Ethnicity? Given the supranational presumption of the European Union, transnational human rights norms remain as the only criteria.)

On January 1, 1990, the same day the Schengen agreement was supposed—but failed—to take effect, the ministers of the then EC-12 made a declaration in Paris noting in part: "We solemnly declare that our objectives shall be achieved in accordance with the international commitments regarding asylum and the humanitarian traditions of our States. . . . [We] undertake to uphold the rights and safeguards of foreigners whose presence there is valid."[45]

The overall thrust of EU developments in the area of immigration—though halting, very slow, constrained by concerns about sovereignty, and institutionally ineffective (compared with the Council of Europe) in dealing with transnational challenges—was to reinforce the order of transnational human rights. As Yasemin Soysal points out, by defining immigration as a policy issue, the EU institutions can legitimately propose laws and policy in this area. This means, in turn, that actors at different levels can make demands on immigration and human rights issues through the EU, thus effectively circumventing the sovereignty of the states.[46]

In turning to the United States we find that international human rights law has made inroads. However, the status of international human rights law is more ambiguous in the United States. American political and national identity has historically been defined in legal and constitutional terms. The idea of a "higher law" that would supersede national law is, consequently, particularly problematic.

5

The United States and the Age of Rights

The founding documents of the United States, the Declaration of Independence and the Constitution, reveal a striking self-consciousness about America's place in the world. The establishment of the United States was at one and the same time the "invention" of a new society and a statement about the world order and America's role in it. Particularly striking in this regard is the first paragraph of the Declaration of Independence, which makes reference to the "separate and equal station" the United States seeks among the family of nations and how "a decent respect to the opinions of mankind requires that [the people of the United States] should declare the causes which impel them to separation."

Thus, the Founding Fathers were launching a revolutionary experiment in domestic social and political relations, but they were also endeavoring to make the country a legitimate enterprise, to be part of the "civilized" world, and to be a nation rooted in international law. The law of nations, Thomas Jefferson stated, was "an integral part . . . of the laws of the land."[1]

The courts assumed from the birth of the Republic that international law was part and parcel of federal common law. The courts had a "duty" to administer "the law of nations." The court in the *Paquete Habana*, the touchstone case concerning the incorporation of international law into American domestic law, noted: "International law is part of our law, and must be ascertained and administered by the courts of justice of appropriate jurisdiction as often as questions of right depending upon it are duly presented for their determination."[2]

Thus, the courts had, and have, a central role in *administering* international law. In a world of sovereign states, that had little import for individuals as such. In such circumstances the courts were more concerned with their scope of jurisdiction and mapping out whose "national interests" were involved. But the courts' role in administering international law becomes critical, and transformative, when individuals and nonstate actors can make claims on states (and even on other nonstate actors) on the basis of international law. Deep structural changes had to take place for this novel status of individuals in international law to arise. Transnational activities, and in particular transnational migration, proved critical in undermining the sharp distinction between national and alien that is intrinsic to a discrete domestic law and to an international law whose object is the state.

While the United States rooted itself in international law, the international human rights that were formulated after World War II drew heavily from American constitutionalism.[3] Yet, the United States or, more specifically, the Senate has been resistant to ratifying international human rights instruments. Even in the face of such resistance international human rights law has made an increasing, if uneven, mark on the United States.

The Constitution and International Law

International law may be applied by the courts in the United States in three ways: (1) through the enforcement of treaties to which the United States is a party; (2) through the application of international customary law; and (3) through the use of international law to inform the process of constitutional and statutory interpretation.

Under Article 6 of the Constitution, "all Treaties made . . . under the Authority of the United States, shall be the supreme Law of the Land." A treaty is ratified by a vote of at least two-thirds of the Senate. Treaties have equal status to federal statutes. If there is a conflict between a federal statute and a self-executing treaty (a treaty that does not require legislation to be implemented) the "later-in-time" rule prevails. No treaty provision, under U.S. domestic law, may be given effect if it is in conflict with the Constitution.

Customary international law has the same status as treaty law, and supersedes all inconsistent local, state, and federal laws. The content of customary international law is inferred from state practice, human rights treaties that over time have become points of reference for international law (even if not ratified by the United States), and even the works of jurists and commentators on the Law of Nations. Genocide, torture, slavery, gross violations of human rights, and systematic racial discrimination are recognized by the United States as lying in the domain of customary international law.[4]

Finally, the Constitution makes possible the use of international law to inform the interpretation of constitutional law such as, for example, the "due process" or "equal protection" clauses.[5]

Because the United States is a party to few human rights treaties, the courts from the 1970s turned to customary international law and to international law as an interpretive device in order to adjudicate cases involving transnational actors.

RESHAPING THE STATE: THE CHANGING ROLE OF INTERNATIONAL LAW

In a case that took place in 1822, *United States v. The La Jeune Eugenie*, Justice Story wrote:

> If a nation were to violate as to its own subjects in its domestic regulation the clearest principles of public law, I do not know that that law has ever held them amenable to the tribunals of other nations for such conduct. *It would be inconsistent with the equality and sovereignty of nations, which admit no common superior.* No nation has ever yet pretended to be the *custos morum* of the whole world; and though abstractedly a particular regulation may violate the law of nations, it may sometimes, in the case of nations, be a wrong without a remedy. (emphasis added)[6]

What is impressive about Story's statement was that it was made in a case in which it was determined that slave trade was an offense against the law of nations. Although certain criminals such as slave traders and pirates were termed *hostes humani generis*, enemies of humanity, nations ignored violations that took place in other countries' sovereign territories. (*The La Jeune Eugenie* determination was, in any event, overturned by the Supreme Court three years later.)[7]

A century later, the principle of sovereignty still reigned supreme. In the *Tinoco* case of 1923, a restored Costa Rican government contended that it could not be bound by the actions of the unconstitutional rule of the minister of war, Tinoco, who seized power in a putsch. Chief Justice Taft stated that Tinoco represented legitimate government simply through his effective control. Transnational human rights concerns did not enter the picture and so the courts have ruled until recently. The judiciary has appealed to international law sparingly, fearful of straying into foreign policy. Jurisdiction, in the classic paradigm, ended at the boundaries of sovereign control.[8]

Similarly, in the area of immigration, the courts have traditionally held that the power and basis for admitting or expelling aliens are concerns of the legislature and beyond judicial review. Constitutional protections were not available for aliens outside the country and aliens in the country have rights that have been merely provisional and contingent. The control of immigration has been considered a cornerstone of sovereignty and thus an area of judicial deference to other branches of government. Until the 1970s, at least, the courts tended to discount international law in the area of immigration. In *Sei Fujii v. California* (1952), for example, the Supreme Court rejected the view that California's Alien Land Law was unenforceable because by discriminating against aliens of Asian origin it violated the U.N. Charter. The court ruled that the charter's provisions were non-self-executing and, consequently, could not supersede state (or federal) law without implementing legislation by Congress.[9]

By the mid-1970s to the early 1980s a shift took place, not without ambivalence but a shift nevertheless, in the courts' approach to international human rights codes. The courts began to focus on these codes not merely as guides to the practice of states but as normative instruments in their own right, as legal regimes for the protection of individuals.

A significant factor in this reevaluation was the perception of a near loss of government control of the migratory flow in this period. Huge numbers of persons could not be accounted for in terms of national legal categories. International human rights instruments do not expressly prohibit distinctions between citizens and aliens, as such, but basic rights are "guaranteed" for all persons within any state's jurisdiction, not just for citizens.[10]

Thus, to take a single international human rights instrument, the Universal Declaration of Human Rights has been cited in seventy-six federal cases from its adoption by the United Nations in 1948 through 1994. Yet a full seventy of those cases—over 90 percent—took place since 1970 (and fifty-nine of those cases occurred since 1980). It is striking that, of those seventy-six cases, 49 percent involved immigration issues and, if we include all refugee cases, the proportion goes up to 54 percent.[11]

Hence international human rights law can fill the lacunae created by transnational migrants and aliens in national legal systems. This is what happened, with some ambivalence, in the U.S. courts. Furthermore, once the use of international human rights instruments became a legitimate avenue for making claims, then that channel became a resource for citizens as well as aliens. The ground rules changed—for everybody.

As early as 1975, aliens making claims on the United States on the basis of international human rights were, in part at least, recognized by the court. It was alleged in a class action suit, *Nguyen Da Yen v. Kissinger,* that the U.S. Immigration Service violated fundamental human rights by, inter alia, subjecting Vietnamese children to involuntary detention. The case was decided on other grounds but the court did note that the illegal seizure and detention of aliens against their will may well be a violation of the law of nations under the Fourth Geneva Convention and the Universal Declaration.[12] The landmark cases that marked the beginnings of a new role for the courts as forums of international law, however, took place in the early 1980s.

In *Fernandez v. Wilkinson* a Cuban national challenged his detention in a U.S. prison as a violation of both the Constitution and international law.[13] Pedro Rodriguez-Fernandez was one of about 13,000 Cubans on the "freedom flotilla" that arrived on June 2, 1980, at Key West, Florida, and sought admission to the United States. Immigration authorities determined that Rodriguez-Fernandez was not "clearly entitled" to land, as he admitted to having a criminal record. In exclusion proceedings he was held to be an "excludable alien" and a deportation order was given. Under a fiction created by the Supreme Court, excludable aliens are legally not in the United States and therefore are not protected under the due process clause of the Constitution. Cuba did not respond to attempts to facilitate his deportation. In September 1980, Rodriguez-Fernandez filed a petition to the federal district for Kansas, where he was imprisoned, charging that his continued confinement without bail or without having been charged with a crime was a violation of the cruel and unusual punishment clause of the Constitution and of international law prohibiting prolonged detention.

The federal district court concluded that the detention violated international law but not the Constitution. The reasoning of the court illustrates how transnational migration creates lacunae that bring international human rights laws to the fore:

> We have declared that [the] indeterminate detention of [the] petitioner . . .
> pending unforeseeable deportation constitutes arbitrary detention. Due
> to the unique legal status of excluded aliens in this country, it is an evil from

which our Constitution and statutory laws afford no protection. Our domestic laws are designed to deter private individuals from harming one another and to protect individuals from abuse by the state. But in the case of unadmitted aliens detained on our soil, but legally deemed to be outside our borders, the machinery of domestic law utterly fails to operate to assure protection.[14]

The court, looking for redress in the area of international law, noted that international rules are binding through treaties or "where it can be established through evidence of a wide practice by states that a customary rule of international law exists."[15] Finding no treaty provision applied in this case, the court turned to customary international rights norms. The court pointed to the U.N. Charter, the Universal Declaration of Human Rights, the European Convention for the Protection of Human Rights, and the International Covenant on Civil and Political Rights in arriving at the decision that customary international law prohibited arbitrary detention. Even though, the court said, "the indeterminate detention of an excluded alien cannot be said to violate the United States Constitution or our statutory laws, it is judicially remedial as a violation of international law."[16] Rodriguez-Fernandez had to be released in the absence of a conviction for a crime, likelihood of absconding, or classification as a security risk.

Of further significance is the references the court made to the other branches of government. The court noted at some length how foreign aid is conditioned in part on the potential recipients record on human rights. The assistant secretary of state for human rights was cited to the effect that foreign governments' records are measured by the standards of the Universal Declaration of Human Rights and other international human rights treaties.[17] In other words, the court reasoned that in demanding other states accede to international human rights law, the United States was itself obligated to that same law. The issue, then, is not so much the scope of the jurisdiction of the state but the state's jurisdictional role.[18] This is a dramatic change in the state's location, its *locus operandi*, in the international order.

The Court of Appeals for the Tenth Circuit affirmed the decision, but on somewhat different grounds. The court in this case used international human rights law to interpret, or fill in for lacunae, in U.S. constitutional provisions. Thus, the circuit court did not dispense with domestic law and rely wholly on customary law, as the district court had, but used international law for "definitional" (rather than "controlling") purposes.[19] In either case, international law played a critical role, even where no binding treaties were found to apply.

Another case, *Filartiga v. Pena-Irala*, decided just before *Fernandez*, is also considered a landmark case in its application of international law.[20] The case is compared with *Brown v. Board of Education* in its importance for "transnational public law."[21]

In *Filartiga*, two Paraguayan nationals charged a former Paraguayan police officer, who was visiting in the United States, with the death by torture of a member of the Filartiga family. Because all parties were aliens, the plaintiffs brought their action under an obscure provision of the First Judiciary Act of 1789, which gave the district courts jurisdiction over civil actions for violations of "the law of nations or a treaty of the United States." Since no treaty applied in the case, the court referred to customary international law's prohibitions against torture. The court cited the U.N. Charter to support the claim that a state's treatment of its own nationals is an issue of international concern. The court also referred to torture-related provisions in the Universal Declaration of Human Rights, Declaration on the Protection of All Persons from Being Subjected to Torture, the American Declaration of the Rights and Duties of Man, the European Convention on Human Rights, and the International Covenant on Civil and Political Rights.[22]

Filartiga attracted considerable attention as it marked a recognition of the expanded importance of international law itself; the provision that was used in the case had very rarely been used before. Furthermore, the case appealed to the *normative* instruments of international law rather than the actual practice of states.[23] The case also pictured a revolutionary role for courts in a world of states, of a court adjudicating not on the basis of national sovereignty but on the basis of international human rights law. We hold, the chief judge in the case, Irving Kaufman, stated "that deliberate torture perpetrated under color of official authority violates universally accepted norms of the international law of human rights, regardless of the nationality of the parties. Thus, whenever an alleged torturer is found . . . within our borders [the law] provides federal jurisdiction."[24]

Thus in this changing order of things, plaintiffs, be they individuals or other nonstate actors, become agents in propagating international law. The state, specifically the courts, mediates between these agents and the international legal order. The state's *locus operandi* is resituated. *Filartiga* is particularly significant in this regard because the case involved citizens from another country for an offense committed in another country. International human rights law presumes that all states have an interest in the observance of human rights by other states. The court, in adjudicating international human rights law, is acting under the aegis of a universal human rights order, and consequently can no longer be viewed as interfering in the domestic affairs of another country. Universal jurisdiction exists when international law holds that an individual is responsible for human rights violations. In such circumstances, the court is not deemed to have imposed its own standards on another country.[25]

The lag and ambivalence in the adoption of international human rights instruments in the United States, compared with the situation in Western Europe, are rooted in American definitions of nationhood.[26] The political definition of nationhood, as opposed to, for example, an emphasis on ethnicity, has led to attempts by the courts in some cases to account for transnational migrants within American constitutionalism. This is demonstrated for example in a case that went before the Supreme Court in 1982, *Plyler v. Doe*. However, the "elasticity" of the Constitution is limited in this regard, for reasons that will be discussed.

International Law, the Constitution, and the American Political Identity

In *Plyler v. Doe* the Supreme Court ruled that a state had to provide the children of illegal aliens free public education.[27] Like *Fernandez*, the courts found themselves faced with a population that did not legally belong in the United States, yet the federal government was evidently unable to deport. Unlike *Fernandez*, however, the courts did not turn to international law, but to the Constitution: the children of the illegal aliens were protected under the equal protection clause.

The plaintiffs had argued in *In re Alien Children Education Litigation*, a related case that was consolidated with *Plyler*, that the right to a free education was recognized in the Universal Declaration of Human Rights, the International Covenant on Economic, Social, and Cultural Rights, and the Declaration of the Rights of the Child, among other international human rights instruments.[28] The court did not accept the customary international law claim, stating that the right to education was an important goal but it had not yet gained the status of customary international law. One could, of course, conclude that the customary international law claim was simply weak. But what is noteworthy is that the court went on to state that the right to education was an appropriate subject for claims *between governments* but not as a customary norm that can be invoked by nonstate actors in U.S. courts.[29] Thus, the court was remaining loyal to the concept of international law as an instrument of state practice. Instead, the access of the children of illegal aliens to public education was accommodated through the Constitution.

The *Plyler* and related cases demonstrate the elasticity of the Constitution and similarly, the reason why, to some extent, international human rights law can be bypassed. The Founders constructed a social contract, called the Constitution, based on the idea of inalienable and natural rights, rights that have no territorial confines.[30] Thus, the Constitution does not by and large state whether it applies only to citizens. The founding documents rather refer to "the people" or "persons." The original Constitution mentions citizenship only as a necessary qualification for the president and for membership in Congress and in the provision that the citizens of each state be entitled to the privileges and immunities of citizens in the several states. Even the Fourteenth Amendment, which established the criteria for citizenship, also provides that no state "shall deprive any *person* of life, liberty, or property without due process of law" (emphasis added). Nor shall any state deny to any *person* within its jurisdiction the "equal protection" of its laws. Even voting is not constitutionally limited to citizens.[31]

The stress on "persons" allows for broad constitutional interpretation about, for example, transnational actors like illegal aliens. Clearly, the *Plyler* decision would have been inconceivable if in the Fourteenth Amendment the equal protection clause was limited to "any citizen" rather than to "any person."

The centrality of the Constitution also explains, in part at least, the decades-long resistance of the Senate to ratify international human rights treaties. The coincidence of the American political and national identities is embodied in the Constitution. In the words of Justice Black, "the United States is entirely a creature of the Constitution."[32] Thus, the incorporation of international human rights law insofar as it, in effect, replaces constitutional law is sociologically problematic for the United States; what *is* the United States without its Constitution, the fountainhead of its political and legal life?

Where definitions of nationhood have been based on blood descent, as in Germany, the state has, paradoxically, turned more quickly to international human rights law to account for transnational migrants. This is because such migrants could not, even in a limited way, be absorbed into the national body politic, unless they were of the same ethnic background. So, for example, although Western European countries as a group shift more quickly than the United States on the issue of international human rights law, there are national differences. As noted earlier, Germany recognized the right of individual petition to the European Court of Human Rights throughout the 1970s and 1980s. France, where nationhood has been defined in more territorial and political terms, accepted such individual and NGO petition rights only in 1981. Germany from 1987 required all German law to be interpreted within the framework of the European Convention on Human Rights by its own courts (see chap. 4). France, like the United States, initially tried to deal with the transnational migration problem domestically.[33]

It would appear, however, that absorbing continuing transnational developments within the constitutional framework will be difficult to sustain. Constitutionally, accepting—and reinforcing—the erosion of the distinction between alien and citizen has its own destructive dialectic; what does the Constitution represent, if not a political and national community? And what is that Constitution if it systematically dismantles the rules for defining that community? As Peter Schuck puts it, "*Plyler's* peculiar vice is that it uses the inherent difficulty of a problem as a justification for making it even more intractable."[34] Thus, it seems clear that the trend toward incorporating international human rights law is inevitable. Indeed, this became more apparent in the Senate's ratification of the International Covenant on Civil and Political Rights in 1992, after fifteen years of blocking any attempts to incorporate this major international human rights instrument into federal law. The Senate's ratification did not include, however, the possibility of individual petition on the basis of the International Covenant on Civil and Political Rights.

Furthermore, the fact that legislative and executive branches of the federal government have increasingly predicated foreign relations since the 1970s on human rights has given further impetus to the use of international human rights instruments. Explicit recognition that such instruments reflect customary international law was evident in the U.S. Memorial to the International Court of Justice in the *Hostages Case*:

> The existence of . . . fundamental human rights for all human beings, *nationals and aliens alike,* and the existence of a corresponding duty on every State to respect and observe them, are now reflected, *inter alia,* in the

Charter of the United Nations, the Universal Declaration of Human Rights and corresponding portions of the International Covenants on Civil and Political Rights, regional conventions and other instruments defining basic human rights. (emphasis added)[35]

More important, the developing case law of the U.S. courts has established some general rules on the enforcement of customary international human rights. First, the individual has a right to invoke customary international human rights law that a court must apply as part of federal law. Second, the international human rights treaties are part of, or the most important evidence as to the content of, customary international law. Third, statements by U.S. government officials are a central source in establishing customary international human rights law.[36]

CALIFORNIA'S PROPOSITION 187: THE RETURN OF *PLYLER*?

The passage of Proposition 187 in California in November 1994 illustrated, paradoxically, the social, political, and legal problems associated with immigration control in the United States. Proposition 187, which was passed by a margin of 59 to 41 percent of the voters, proposed sanctions for the manufacture, sale, or use of fraudulent residency or citizenship documents and excluded illegal aliens from public social services or benefits and from publicly funded health care (except in emergencies). Furthermore, illegal aliens were to be barred from public elementary and secondary schools and from public postsecondary education, including California's public universities. Education and health officials would have to report to the immigration authorities any person who they knew or suspected was an illegal alien.[37]

Although the measure was roundly supported by the voters, state and federal judges barred the proposition from taking effect, with the exception of the fraudulent documents section (which largely duplicated federal laws), after ethnic, civil rights, and local government groups challenged its constitutionality. Many school and health officials said they would refuse to enforce the proposition in any event. Interestingly, most of the lawsuits, focusing on the schools issue, based their challenge of Proposition 187's constitutionality on the *Plyler* precedent. (In a sense, *Plyler* contributed to the proposition in the first place: it was generally agreed on both sides of the controversy that California was providing education to roughly 308,000 illegal immigrants, at an estimated annual cost of $1.4 billion dollars, *because* of the legal precedent set by the *Plyler* case. The apparent cost of illegal aliens to the taxpayer was one stated reason for the proposition.) Lawyers suggested that the blocked provisions would remain tied up at the very least for two to three years until they reached the U.S. Supreme Court; only at that point could *Plyler* be, possibly, turned over.[38]

The proposition nevertheless generated intense national interest and brought immigration to the center of public debate once more. Immigration appeared to be an issue that would carry through to the 1996 presidential election with public pressure yet again, almost a decade after IRCA, to control illegal immigration. In a national poll shortly after the passage of Proposition 187 some 58 percent of respondents favored a law in their respective states similar to Proposition 187, a law that would "stop providing health benefits and public education to illegal immigrants, including children." In a different national poll, 58 percent also said they closely or very closely followed news stories about Proposition 187.[39]

However, Proposition 187 curiously demonstrated the permanence of large noncitizen populations and the devaluation of citizenship. The proposition reinforced the notion that the status of legal residents who are not citizens and the status of citizens are essentially the same in that the proposition's wording is designed to carefully target only illegal immigrants. Furthermore, the proposition ironically showed the intractability of the illegal immigration problem: how could hundreds of thousands of children be forced into the streets, or hundreds of thousands of illegal immigrants be denied public health services, without public health and public safety ramifications? Given the even worse economic conditions in the home countries of the great majority of illegal immigrants, the hoped for "self-reparation" would be limited at best.

Conclusion

This discussion on Western Europe and the United States has concentrated almost exclusively on the role of the courts. This is important because the courts have historically played a central role in social and political transformation. Furthermore, we witness today a dramatic upsurge in constitutional politics that has brought the courts to center stage not only in the United States but in Western Europe. Because the legislative and executive have to pay increasing attention to the courts in Western Europe as well as in the United States, the judiciary has a larger political significance. Commentators observe how regime legitimacy has come to rest on the courts, focusing above all on human rights. It has been noted that there has been "a stealthy, almost invisible growth of constitutional rights and judicial claims of authority."[40]

Perhaps most notable, however, is that the courts are more evocative of the character and direction of contemporary social and political change. On the most straightforward level, the courts' approach to law delineates the contours of political and social activity. By deferring to the executive and legislative entities of government "at the water's edge," at the national boundaries, in areas such as foreign relations and immigration, the court recognizes the state as sovereign. The court is deferring to the branches of government that represent the people and that incorporate a free and self-governing nation in the international arena. The legislative and executive are the forums that are most expressive of national self-determination. The courts, domestically, adjudicate nationally inspired rules and laws. In the new world, however, the courts pay increasing attention to international—indeed, transnational—laws and norms. Principles of national self-determination, national interest, the scope of a court's jurisdiction, and sovereignty become secondary. Even borders are not sacrosanct and have to be understood in a new light.[41]

The changing modus operandi of the courts reveals, in other words, that not only has one piece of the puzzle been cut differently, but all the pieces have to be recut accordingly. The court's role is a metaphor for the evolving place of the state in the new world: the state is now a forum where transnational laws and norms are administered, mediated, and enforced. The courts, through realizing and enforcing international human rights instruments, may have indeed become the midwives of a new world order. The pieces of the puzzle have not only changed shape. The picture that has been built up, piece by piece, is different from the one promised on the box.

Insofar as the state has to take account of international human rights vis-à-vis all its residents, citizen and noncitizen, then the premise that an individual or group of people has to "belong" to a territorially bounded nation in order to enjoy rights is superseded or at least diluted. Individuals and nonstate groups, in making claims on the state in terms of international human rights, can become transnational actors on the international stage. This suggests that significant institutional reformations are taking place.

6

States without Nations

History has become mobilized; it is accelerating,
even overheating. The new problems are shifting
old perspectives and, what is more important,
opening up new perspectives for the future [and
new] points of view that restore our ability to
perceive alternative courses of action.

JÜRGEN HABERMAS

The separation of "rights" from "belonging," of membership in the state from membership in the nation, of the national home from the state, has a larger political and global significance than, say, immigration policy per se.[1] The state always lay at the intersection of international and domestic politics; as notions of statehood and nationhood evolve, so must conceptions of international community and institutions, of the domestic and international roles of the state, and of the place of nonstate groups be reevaluated.

This chapter begins by considering the Organization for Security and Cooperation in Europe (OSCE) and its special role in shaping the emerging political framework and in its function as a symbol of a nascent transatlantic community. As states become increasingly "constituted" by international human rights codes, they will act in concert with other like-minded states—in this sense, the OSCE represents a Euro-Atlantic community. It is through the framework of the OSCE that the most ambitious and concerted effort is being made not only to define the post–cold war order but also to articulate the changing character of, and ties between, international institutions, the state, and nonstate groups. Although the fall of the Soviet Union acted as a catalyst for this effort, the OSCE documents from 1990 recognize longer-term developments in shaping the post–cold war world.[2] Then, in an exploratory fashion and extrapolating somewhat from contemporary developments, the chapter considers the changing character of the state in both its domestic and international dimensions.

The Organization for Security and Cooperation in Europe

The OSCE articulates and institutionalizes on a community-wide level three critical elements alluded to in the previous chapters: (1) human rights are the basis of state legitimacy; (2) the source of state authority is shifting to a transnational level; (3) the state, paradoxically, becomes ever more important as the bureaucratic apparatus of this emerging order. Thus, the OSCE notes approvingly of the member states' expansion that has already taken place in order to ensure the human rights of its residents and, furthermore, gives legal encouragement for further growth of the state apparatus. Such an expansion of the state is implicit in its mandate to facilitate the "positive" (human) rights of citizen and noncitizen alike.

The OSCE has come to signify the existence of a Euro-Atlantic Community, and its basis, its very reason for being, is the institution of human rights. The Euro-Atlantic community includes North America and the European Union with an increasing number of countries in Eastern Europe and in the former Soviet Union. The OSCE is not the only or necessarily the most effective institution in advancing international human rights. Other regional and international institutions are in many respects more effective. Nor does the OSCE have the extensive institutional formation of, say, the European Union. Rather the OSCE is symbolically and institutionally the intersection of a variety of organizations with more specific and narrowly defined goals; the OSCE embodies their larger purpose and commonality. The OSCE is the node ("the point that stands still") that binds the larger universe of organizations and states. (Thus NATO, the Western European Union, the Council of Europe, and the European Bank for Reconstruction and Development, among other groups, partake in OSCE meetings.) The OSCE's primary significance is as a political entity, delimiting a new community and defining new purposes for government.[3]

The Conference on Security and Cooperation in Europe (CSCE) was created by the Helsinki Final Act in 1975.[4] At first a diplomatic forum to alleviate tensions between East and West, the now named OSCE (since the 1994 Budapest meeting of the organization) has been transformed into an institution in which political legitimacy is reserved only for states that, it was agreed at the organization's Copenhagen human dimension meeting in June 1990, "recognize pluralistic democracy and the rule of the law are essential for ensuring all human rights and fundamental freedoms." States are required to translate the political commitments of the OSCE into domestic laws and policies.[5]

The OSCE departs from the framework of traditional state-centric diplomatic documents, and did so from its founding in Helsinki. The participants do not represent geographic regions, indicating the OSCE's universal significance. No reference is made to alliances or distinctions between major powers and small states. The OSCE is of universal significance in another sense; it is an instrument for nongovernmental organizations, intergovernmental organizations, civic groups, individuals, and others to draw on in making human rights claims, not just for states. Thus, the Helsinki Final Act speaks of "dissemination" of its provisions and the requirement to make the provisions "known as widely as possible." The CSCE/OSCE from the beginning was not an agreement simply for states. The OSCE is consequently of great symbolic as well as practical significance, but in functional terms it complements regional and national institutions (including the states themselves) in realizing the new international constitutional order, based on human rights.[6]

Individual states do remain central, however, in that the organization has been run largely on the basis of consensus. A single member can veto any resolution. At the Budapest meeting in 1994, for example, Russia blocked approval of a declaration that condemned Bosnian Serbs for their assault on the "safe area" of Bihac and for the "ethnic cleansing" in all of Bosnia.

STATE LEGITIMACY

In the process of articulating, "organizing," and repackaging the global present and future, the OSCE meeting in Paris deserves special attention. The Charter of Paris for a New Europe, signed by the then thirty-four members of the CSCE on November 21, 1990, not only formally marked the end of the cold war but also charted the path ahead. In this respect, it served as an important marker in the ongoing paradigmatic and systemic movement away from notions of state sovereignty. What the principle of *cuius regio, eius religio* was to the Peace of Westphalia, so human rights were to the Charter of Paris; an organizing principle of domestic and international politics in aspiration and, to an increasing degree, in practice as well.[7] The Council of Europe, the parent body of the European Convention on Human Rights, is repeatedly referred to in OSCE documents to illustrate, as it were, that human rights are now a central part of the political fabric in the West.

Under the heading, "A New Era of Democracy, Peace and Unity," the charter self-consciously proclaimed the end of one era and the beginning of another:

> We, the Heads of State or Government [of the CSCE] have assembled in Paris at a time of profound change and historic expectations. The era of confrontation and division of Europe has ended. . . .
>
> Europe is liberating itself from the legacy of the past. The courage of men and women, the strength of the will of the peoples and the power of the ideas of the Helsinki Final Act have opened a new era. . . .
>
> Ours is a time for fulfilling the hopes and expectations our peoples have cherished for decades: steadfast commitment to democracy based on human rights and fundamental freedoms; prosperity through economic liberty and social justice; and equal security for all our countries.

The charter then goes on to state that human rights are to be the basic purpose of government:

> Human rights and fundamental freedoms are the birthright of all human beings, are inalienable and guaranteed by law. Their protection and promotion are the first responsibility of government. Respect for them is an essential safeguard against an over-mighty state. Their observance and full exercise are the foundation of freedom, justice and peace.[8]

One practical change the OSCE effected was that in order for a state to join the Euro-Atlantic community it had to demonstrate its political and social practices were in accordance with international human rights law. This was of dramatic importance as the OSCE provided the blueprint to statehood for all the old-new countries emerging in Eastern Europe and the Soviet Union. James Baker, U.S. secretary of state, noted about the Copenhagen meeting of the OSCE that took place in June 1990:

> The norms of conduct adopted at Copenhagen are an important means of holding governments accountable for the treatment that they accord their citizens. *The Copenhagen provisions serve as clear guidelines for the nations now making difficult transitions to democracy and reform.* They open up national elections in all CSCE countries to observers from other CSCE countries. And they point the way to resolving human rights issues that remain causes of concern in Central and Eastern Europe and in the Soviet Union. (emphasis added)[9]

Although human rights are a central concern from the Helsinki Accords, their role as the basis of international legitimacy of states is accentuated from the Copenhagen and Paris meetings. In addition to the Paris charter's references to government and human rights, in the Prague meeting in 1992, for example, the role of the OSCE "in fostering democratic development and fully integrating participating States into the network of shared [OSCE] values" is stressed.[10] Member states are called on to accede to the International Covenants of Civil and Political Rights and of Economic, Social, and Cultural Rights if they have not already done so.[11] Other human rights are specifically mentioned, such as the right of movement, communication, and association.[12]

THE SHIFTING LOCUS OF STATE AUTHORITY

The institutional framework and the discourse associated with the OSCE also suggest that the expansion of human rights has transcended the boundaries of the state per se. In other words, under the OSCE human rights are no longer a secondary theme in the business of states.

Different elements in the organization's documents indicate the shifting source of state authority. Now anyone whose human rights have been violated shall have access to remedies not only on the national level but on the international and regional levels as well. The state itself is required to follow (and thus become accountable to) international human rights instruments—to the extent of incorporating international human rights into national law. The OSCE calls upon member states to permit the presence of foreign observers at elections. States are required to permit and facilitate cross-border and transnational contacts between nongovernment associations and international organizations to promote human rights. Under the OSCE individuals and groups may turn to international bodies with information on human rights abuses. The OSCE promotes intersocietal cooperation between political groups and encourages the central role of the Council of Europe.[13]

The critical role of an independent judiciary for the advancement of international human rights is repeatedly stressed.[14] Member states of the OSCE accept and facilitate "Rapporteur Missions" to report on that state's progress in implementing OSCE commitments. Political and military leaders are held personally responsible for any human rights violations they oversee.[15]

Because the OSCE recognizes and promotes the role of nongovernment groups as agents of the international human rights order, such groups have direct access to the OSCE institutions. (Similarly, European and transatlantic groups, like NATO, the Council of Europe, and the Western European Union, are called upon to contribute in the areas where they have expertise.) In the Moscow document, the member states commit themselves to recognize all self-described NGOs. They will strengthen "modalities for contacts" between such groups and governments; facilitate visits by NGOs from other OSCE countries to observe human rights compliance; and allow these nongovernmental groups to communicate their findings to other governments and to the OSCE. NGOs are to be also invited to OSCE meetings.[16]

THE EXPANDING STATE BUREAUCRACY

While the state's sovereignty is severely curtailed in that its basis of legitimacy is coming to rest on international human rights and its source of authority is the transnational human rights order, the state bureaucracy shows every sign of further expansion—an expansion aided and abetted by the OSCE as well as other international human rights instruments.

The *state itself*, the Copenhagen document recognized, is the critical mechanism in advancing human rights. A striking dialectic becomes evident. As the states' source of authority becomes transnational, its bureaucratic importance grows.[17] The state apparatus expands in order to fulfill its mandate to promote and facilitate human rights, particularly positive rights. Negative rights demand the state refrain from interfering in, say, the right to privacy. Positive rights demand action by the state in, for example, "affirmative action" policies. The state, then, is not antithetical to the emerging transnational human rights order but an essential and intrinsic element of that order.[18]

The expansion of the state's role is implicit in an extensive list of both general and specific requirements on states designed to advance human rights. In general the states are called on "to foster" democratic culture in education, the media, religious groups and civic organizations, professions, political parties and public administration, and the armed forces and the police.[19] An example of a more specific demand, from the Moscow document, requires that states seek not only de jure but de facto equality between men and women. Thus, the member states must "establish or strengthen national machinery . . . for the advancement of women in order to ensure that programs and policies are assessed for their impact on women." States must implement measures "to ensure full economic opportunity for women, including non-discriminatory employment policies and practices, equal access to education and training, and measures to facilitate combining employment with family responsibilities." The full participation of women in political and public life is to be actively promoted. Educational curricula should, according to international human rights norms as defined by the OSCE, promote the equality of women, including in nontraditional areas. States are required to collect data to monitor if the situation of women is improving—a clear support for affirmative action-type policies. Similar requirements are made for other categories of persons, such as the disabled.[20] The expanding role of the state is most striking—in terms not only of legal requirements but of actual state practice—in the areas of foreign, minority, and migrant populations.

"NATIONAL MINORITIES"

Foreign populations, it has been argued all along, have played an important role in the growing importance of international human rights as transnational persons most precisely fit the notion of "personhood" that transcends the more familiar national-alien distinction. Such populations, in the context of the OSCE as in other cases, act as a impetus for the adoption of international human rights codes.[21]

National minorities have traditionally referred to long-standing groups who have often had an antagonistic relationship with the majority such as, for example, the Basques in Spain. However, with the large movements of people in the postwar period, including migrants, the term has greater legal and political implications. (Interestingly, the CSCE Meeting of Experts on National Minorities emphasizes that not all "ethnic, cultural, linguistic or religious differences" constitute national minorities.[22] This point is apparently designed to stress the "voluntarist" character of all groups and, in addition, to demarcate national minorities and other transnational populations from the more traditional "domestic" minorities such as African-Americans or Greek-Americans.)

The OSCE, as noted earlier, institutionalizes on a transatlantic level human rights as the basis of state legitimacy, the shift in the source of state authority to a transnational level, and, finally, the growth of the state apparatus in its role as caretaker of human rights. Not surprisingly, all three dimensions are accentuated and reinforced by the permanent and growing presence of noncitizens.

Nationality, the OSCE in effect states (in the context of minority populations), is a human right. Such rights are not only "domestic" but international: "Issues concerning national minorities, as well as compliance with international obligations and commitments concerning the rights of persons belonging to them, *are matters of legitimate international concern* and consequently do not constitute exclusively an internal affair of the respective State" (emphasis added).[23] Elsewhere, in the Copenhagen document, it is noted that member states, "in their efforts to protect and promote the rights of persons belonging to national minorities, will fully respect their undertakings under existing human rights conventions and other relevant human rights instruments and consider adhering to the relevant conventions, if they have not yet done so, including those providing for the right of complaint by individuals."[24]

A graphic illustration of the way nationality has been recast from a principle of national self-determination to a principle of nationality as a human right, and a striking example of the ability of the OSCE and the Council of Europe to shape domestic and international relations, is how Latvia amended its citizenship law. Latvia passed a citizenship law that would have had the effect of denying citizenship to the vast majority of Russians who live in Latvia. The Russian population makes up about 36 percent of Latvia's total population. Responding more to pressure from the OSCE and the Council of Europe, the parent body of the European Court of Human Rights, than to pressure from Russia itself, Latvia shortly thereafter, in July 1994, amended the law such that now almost all denizens of Latvia, including Russians, will be naturalized by the year 2000.[25]

The use of external observers is also encouraged to observe compliance in the area of international human rights for national minorities. The OSCE states accept that foreign groups can organize and advocate their cause transnationally, that promotion of minority identities involves in part cross-border ties, and that such ethnic groups are transnational agents in a larger human rights order. (Curiously, what is "cross-border" is no longer viewed as "cross-cultural." That is, cross-cultural ties can now be between domestic groups, whereas cultural groups in many cases unite across borders.)[26]

Most remarkable, however, is the extent to which the state apparatus is to be expanded to ensure the human rights of foreign populations and, indeed, the extent to which a number of state bureaucracies already have expanded to take account of such populations' human rights.

The Meeting of Experts on National Minorities approvingly notes the measures that have already been undertaken by a number of states and sets them up as models for the Euro-Atlantic community as a whole. Those actions (some of which were discussed in chap. 2), involving expanded state bureaucracies, include political and administrative measures:

—advisory and decision-making bodies in which minorities are represented, in particular with regard to education, culture and religion;

—elected bodies and assemblies of national minority affairs;

—local and autonomous administration . . . including the existence of consultative, legislative and executive bodies chosen through free and periodic elections;

—self-administration by a national minority of aspects concerning its identity in situations where autonomy on a territorial basis does not apply;

—decentralized or local forms of government . . .;

—creation of government research agencies to review legislation and disseminate information related to equal rights and non-discrimination;

—governmental assistance [to address local] discriminatory practices.[27]

International arrangements such as bilateral or multilateral agreements and other arrangements that promote national minorities are also cited by the OSCE. Education for foreign populations is a central feature and measures already undertaken by some states include providing education in the mother tongue, recognizing foreign diplomas, providing financial and technical assistance, and teaching minority languages to the general public.[28]

The OSCE also advocates further measures to ensure the human rights of foreign populations, creating the legal space and the normative pressure for further state expansion. States "will create conditions" to ensure equal opportunity in public life, in the economic sphere, and in "the building of their societies." Human rights are to be respected on a non-discriminatory basis. In compliance with the Copenhagen document, states are called on to provide a "broad array" of judicial and administrative remedies for redress of grievances. States must promote the preservation of the culture and heritage of minority populations and create the conditions for the promotion of such identities. States have to act to constrain the "incitement to violence" that is rooted in ethnic, religious, or anti-Semitic prejudice. Data on such acts must be published. The media will be "assisted" in taking account of ethnic and cultural differences.[29] Protections of a "positive" character specific to migrants are also noted.[30]

In a sentence that summarizes and encapsulates recent developments and frames the future, it is noted that member states of the OSCE "affirm that persons belonging to a national minority will enjoy the same rights and have the same duties of citizenship as the rest of the population." Reflecting a fundamental shift away from aspirations for unitary states and "melting pots," attempts at the assimilation of minority populations are deemed unacceptable. The imagery, though not explicitly stated, is rather of a consociational or a "multicultural" form of governance. The statement is also significant in that national minorities are to have the same *duties* as well as the same rights as citizens: this illustrates, again, the dialectical relationship between transnational human rights and the state. National minorities, including migrants and other aliens, have certain obligations to the state. The state, under the aegis of international human rights instruments, can thus make demands of aliens to support the state (through, for example, taxes and even military service).[31]

"We are witnessing a sea change in international law," writes Thomas Franck, the scholar of international human rights law, "as a result of which the legitimacy of each government someday will be measured definitively by international rules and processes." He goes on to note that we "are not quite there, but we can see the outlines of this new world in which the citizens of each state will look to international law and organization to guarantee democratic entitlement."[32] When we view the state in both its domestic and international facets in this emerging new world, we observe it has two sets of boundaries, inner and outer, or internal and external. The state, internally, is the institutional mechanism and forum for the international constitutional order within its administrative area—the state is accountable for the human rights and welfare of its residents. The state's external borders are those of the Euro-Atlantic community, borders that the state, in concert with other member states, defends, protects—and extends. Drawing on the developments described up to now, and purposely extrapolating these developments forward, we ask, in an exploratory fashion, What *is* the shape of this evolving "world"?

Charting a New Terrain

A veritable transformation has taken place in the world order such that, at least at the core of that order, the Euro-Atlantic community, the idiom and practice of state sovereignty and national self-determination are becoming problematic.[33] It is time to dispense with those concepts, at least for analytical purposes, as they confuse understanding of the new international order.

States are the "pillars" of the Euro-Atlantic community in that states regulate and institute the system of rules that constitute the community. In realpolitik terms, states are the carriers of the instruments of violence. Thus, in the area of "collective security" certain more powerful states may play a more salient role. However, there are revolutionary changes in the making, compared with the system of states known up to now. The state is becoming accountable to, and legitimated by, the transnational human rights order. In this respect the state changes not only in form but in function as well. The state's jurisdictional and judicial role is increasingly defined by, and predicated on, that transnational order. The state is, ontologically speaking, an "indiscrete" element of that order. The raison d'être of this constitutional order is not *raison d'état* but the order itself, namely human rights. The purposes and practices of the state are less and less directed toward or governed by the protection of its own national borders or interests. The state is increasingly committed to a broader entity, of which it is now an intrinsic element, the Euro-Atlantic community. The state is not enclosed but tied to a set of community-wide concerns. The boundaries of that community are fluid as potentially more states can be drawn into its ambit.

The changed role of the state can be illustrated by developing two dimensions: the state as a domestic entity, and the international role of the state. (The terms *domestic* and *international* [or *foreign*] are used in a relative sense; the social and political division implied by such terms is clearly less apt in the new international arrangement.)

THE DOMESTIC FACE OF THE NEW STATE

The evolving domestic role of the state can be illustrated by considering the implications of a "recast" nationality. Formerly, the concept of nationality was designed to reinforce state sovereignty and the principle of self-determination. Classically, the individual had a legal status only insofar as he or she had a nationality, an attachment to a territory that is recognized by the sovereign state concerned. This concept of nationality is being turned on its head.

Recast, nationality is a way of making the state itself accountable for the rights and the welfare of its residents, on the basis of international human rights codes. The individual is the object of international institutions and law, whereas the state is the forum and the institutional mechanism for enforcing these rights.

The question, then, is, When is a state responsible for an individual? Or, conversely, When can an individual (or an NGO) make claims on a state?

An individual has to establish a connection to a state's territory. Herein, the rationale of border control in the new international order comes up. In the traditional nation-state, border control is inherent in the practice of national self-determination. By determining who may, and who may not, enter, reside, and naturalize in a country, the state establishes the "community of character," that is, the defining elements of its nationhood. Clearly, this rationale breaks down in the reconfigured state.

Instead, in the new international order attachment to a territory is established on the basis of universal and transnational (as opposed to particularistic and national) criteria.[34] For example, refugees must be admitted or rejected on the basis of universal (even if very restrictive) criteria, *not* on the basis of race, national origin, political sympathies, and the like.[35] Similarly deportations and extraditions must be based on universal criteria. Attachments to a territory are established through social relationships, such as direct family ties, not in terms of a sovereign state's self-defined interests.[36]

The individual's ties to the state, consequently, are defined more and more by international human rights codes, not by the state as such.

As a result, with massive migration movements, multiple state memberships, transnational economic ties, ethnic dispersion, and social and political movements with transnational concerns (such as the environment), we have, in many cases, a set of transnational, cross-cutting links where individuals and NGOs can make claims on different states, each accountable to similar international human rights codes.

Individuals and NGOs will thus have a variety of ties that bring them into stronger or weaker contact with different states.[37] American workers in a Honda plant in Ohio will have one set of ties with the U.S. government and a different set of ties with Japan. The Honda executives, similarly, will have a differing set of ties with the two governments, probably of reverse order (in closeness of ties) than the American workers.[38] NGOs, such as migrant support groups or ethnic associations, are in contact with a number of states in pursuing the interests of their "constituents."

Transnational issues often arise. Claims can be made on one state for the impact of an activity in that state on another territory. Thus, claims may be made, for example, for environmental damage that resulted from pollution arising in one country but affecting another. Environmental groups have made claims for Indians in Brazil whose lives have been disrupted by development projects of Western companies.[39]

As states are mechanisms of a broader constitutional order, an NGO in one state can make claims on another state with regard to the acts of private parties. In other words, private violations of international human rights can be challenged transnationally. A Jewish organization in London, for example, can make claims on the Russian government to restrain the anti-Semitic activities of the Russian nationalist Pamyat movement, on the basis of the OSCE. International prohibitions of slavery, genocide, or hostage taking apply to private groups and persons as well as to states.[40]

The increasing application of international human rights law to violations between private parties demonstrates the changing links between international institutions, states, and NGOs or individuals. This development illustrates the shift of the state as a political expression of nationhood to a regulative mechanism of a broader constitutional order; thus a state can be accountable to a foreign NGO, under international human rights codes, and be required to restrain its own domestic groups! Obligations are now imposed on the state in terms of its own nationals—not only to uphold their human rights but to ensure that they do not violate the transnational codes to which the state is now accountable.

Thus, as international institutions and laws focus more on NGOs and individuals, instead of states, so NGOs and individuals become the dynamic, the agents that propagate, reproduce, and interpret the premises of the international order itself.[41] The state, formerly *the* actor in international relations, now becomes the forum or mechanism that binds together the nonstate associations and the set of rules that make up the international order.[42]

The state, consequently, has become a forum for competing claims and beliefs.[43] The state is no longer projected as the embodiment of the "general will" of a people or nation, but is now a forum for, so to speak, "competing wills," often concerning transnational associations and issues. Contested issues are adjudicated on the basis of the merits of the case, as defined by international human rights codes, and not on the basis of "national interest" or how the state defines its scope of jurisdiction.[44]

It is remarkable how, as individuals and NGOs become the objects of international institutions and law, so NGOs can even act on such institutions directly. A striking example of this phenomenon was the argument over abortion that took place at the U.N. population conference in Cairo in September 1994. Catholic, Muslim, and feminist nongovernmental groups, as well as the Vatican and different states, parried over the

meaning and extent of "reproductive rights." With the growing importance of international human rights in shaping domestic issues, domestic
conflicts "go global" as different groups seek to shape evolving notions of
human rights.[45] In this respect, human rights are not conservative or
liberal as such; just as, say, the U.S. Constitution is open to, within limits,
varying interpretations, so the parameters of human rights are being
contended.

THE STATE AS AN INTERNATIONAL ENTITY

States are more constrained domestically in the new international
order than was the case in the system of sovereign states. International
human rights codes increasingly determine the character of the state's ties
with its own nationals, rather than the state itself defining the basis of
those ties, as has traditionally been the case. In contrast to past practice,
the way the state treats its own nationals is more and more a matter of
international concern. International intervention in the name of human
rights is, as a result, increasingly legitimate. Thus the new state is more
constrained vertically, and less restrained horizontally, than has been the
case up to now.

States in the Euro-Atlantic community whose legitimacy—indeed,
their very existence—is predicated on international human rights codes
conduct relations with states outside the community on the basis of those
same human rights codes. This phenomenon began to be institutionalized, interestingly, in the mid-1970s and has become increasingly significant ever since. From that period military and economic aid was made
contingent on the observation of internationally recognized human rights.
Such aid can be and often is cut off when recipient countries engage in a
"consistent pattern of gross violations," to use the phrase of a U.N.
resolution that was adopted by the United States, among others.[46] Rulings
by international institutions, such as the Inter-American Court of Human
Rights, are taken into account in assessing human rights records.

International financial institutions that are supported by the European
Union and the United States, such as the World Bank and the European
Bank for Reconstruction and Development, have introduced human
rights criteria into their decision-making process.

Special human rights departments have been set up in foreign minis-
tries to monitor human rights records of other countries. These human
rights departments use human rights groups, such as Amnesty International and Human Rights Watch, in their consultations (yet another

avenue for international NGOs to use state forums to advance international codes). Although of limited influence in the 1970s when first established, these human rights offices are now very consequential; few countries can consistently violate human rights without suffering diplomatic consequences.[47]

The Bureau of Human Rights and Humanitarian Affairs in the U.S. Department of State, for example, is required to submit to Congress human rights reports on all countries that receive American assistance or are members of the United Nations. Human rights officers have been appointed to the five geographic offices of the Department of State to inform all levels of foreign policy making. In the 1988 annual report on human rights, some 169 countries were being surveyed. In the words of the 1988 report, "human rights concerns [are] an integral part of the State Department's . . . daily decision-making."[48]

This development also reflects changes in international law that legitimate intervention when a state violates human rights. "If by violating the human rights of its nationals," writes Theodor Meron, summing up the legal approach on the matter, "a state offends the general international legal order, and thereby also equally offends every other state, then every state has the necessary standing to bring an action against those that perpetrate violations of norms of international human rights."[49] Indeed, we are likely to see increasingly active forms of intervention in the area of human rights, not only cutoffs in aid but other sanctions as well. In the crisis in the former Yugoslavia, the West, for example, brought human rights expressly to the fore as a sine qua non for recognition, though active military intervention was initially limited.[50]

The Russian attack on Chechnya, a region under Russian jurisdiction where independence-minded Chechens were rebelling, was viewed by many as a serious blow to the emerging security "architecture" in the Euro-Atlantic community. The attack, which escalated quickly in January 1995, was undertaken by a central member of the OSCE. The attack resulted in extensive civilian casualties. Furthermore, the attack quickly followed fissures that had developed between Russia and other members of the OSCE at the Budapest meeting of that organization. But, paradoxically, in some respects the Chechnya conflict actually raised the profile of, and even strengthened, the OSCE and the principle of human rights as a basis for intervention. The question is not so much that the norms of the Euro-Atlantic community were violated; norms of all kinds are violated every day. The question is what is the response to such violations and what sanctions are imposed to signal that those norms are tangible and "authentic" and that there are negative consequences for violating them.

The Chechnya issue became defined through the prism of international human rights, rather than as an "internal issue" of Russia or a sovereignty question. The very use of the OSCE as the institution to represent the collective response of the Euro-Atlantic community to the crisis gave note of the importance of human rights and the legitimacy of international involvement in what once would have been considered an internal affair of a sovereign country. The OSCE was so central in this process that it served as the explicit institutional channel for the response of the EU and individual countries to the crisis, illustrating how it has become the institutional symbol of the Euro-Atlantic community. An international delegation, under the auspices of the OSCE, was sent to investigate possible human rights violations by both sides in Chechnya.

Active military intervention in Russia by, say, NATO was clearly out of the question. But once human rights became the point of reference, the members of the Euro-Atlantic states came under increasing pressure to impose sanctions of one kind or another. Aside from the condemnations that, inter alia, the Russian action was "out of line with European norms," by February 1995 concrete steps were beginning to be taken as well. The EU delayed implementing a partnership agreement that was designed to lead to a Russia-EU free trade agreement, encourage private companies from the EU to invest in Russia, and to establish a regular channel of communication between Moscow and Brussels. Strong pressure was being applied by different government officials and by NGOs like Human Rights Watch to suspend Russia's planned accession to the Council of Europe. OSCE ministers gave barely veiled threats to halt aid to Russia as well.[51]

COLLECTIVE SECURITY

The nation-state has the ultimate purpose of representing and protecting a nation on the international stage. Such a state is enclosed, its purposes defined by its national borders and interests. Such a state enters into alliances, engages in "balance-of-power" politics and other such exercises, but all such practices are designed, ultimately, to ensure the independence and sovereignty of the state. This is not simply an exercise of "power" as the cruder theorists of realpolitik would have us believe, but balance-of-power practices are essential institutional means of upholding the principle of national self-determination. Logically independence can be guaranteed only by being able to defend oneself from hostile forces.

The new state, on the other hand, is increasingly a regulative mechanism of a wider community and set of ideas and beliefs. The state, rooted in a *raison* that transcends national self-determination (of a territorial character), finds its practices change as well. The state's protective mission is no longer enclosed, but is defined by the community of which it is an intrinsic part. Being a part of that community, the state no longer acts unilaterally or in coalition with other states as the balance of power demands. The state acts as a subunit of a wider order; security is inherently a collective concern. "Collective security" is the basis on which threats, external and internal, are to be met.

Active military intervention is legitimate only through collective agreements, which are generally reached through international or regional institutions. The objective of such intervention should be in support of democracy and human rights or, at the very least, humanitarian.[52] Thus the institutional context for the exercise of power shifts away from sovereign states. Targets of such use of power can legitimately be countries that are gross violators of human rights and democratic norms. "Power balances, nuclear deterrence, and threats of retaliation retain meaningful roles," Emanual Adler writes, "but only in thought about the community as a whole, vis-à-vis other political units."[53] Collective security, in the new international constitutional order, is distinct from alliances; the security framework is predicated on a broader community. It is not a creation of sovereign states. In other words, collective security serves the goals of the overarching community, not the individual units or states per se.[54] Nevertheless, since historically certain states have stronger military forces, they may play a more salient role in security issues. But such a role will always come under the aegis of the Euro-Atlantic community (and its allies), and other international institutions, as a collective whole.

The Euro-Atlantic community's principle of collective security is increasingly recognized as the "frame" within which the new world is interpreted. Two important speeches in this regard were given by Secretary of State James Baker, on June 18, 1991, to the Aspen Institute and, on April 21, 1992, to the Chicago Council on Foreign Relations. These two speeches served to articulate the form the world order was taking and the centrality in that order of a new entity—the Euro-Atlantic community. In these speeches Baker hailed the emergence of the Euro-Atlantic community, a community "based upon the concept of individual political rights and economic liberty." The United States, Baker said, could not act as a lone superpower. Rather a "democratic peace" would be built around the world through "collective engagement." He cited the Gulf War and Western assistance programs for Eastern Europe and the former Soviet republics as examples of collective engagement.[55]

Predictions that the end of a bipolar balance between the East and West blocs would be followed by multipolar balances of power have not been borne out. Moreover, the balance-of-power concept does not appear to have a central role in the new international order. The Euro-Atlantic community is a dynamic one, pushing at its edges to draw more states into its orbit and into an emerging international constitutional order based on human rights. Two factors underlie this dynamic. First, the *raison* of the Euro-Atlantic community rests in transnational human rights. By definition those human rights are universally applicable and they include countries outside the Euro-Atlantic sphere. "We stand ready," the Charter of Paris proclaims, "to join with any and all States in common efforts to protect and advance the community of fundamental human values."[56]

Second, the growing transnational links and growing importance of NGOs of all kinds cut across the boundaries of the Euro-Atlantic community. Thus, not only is global interdependence enhanced, but the NGOs act as pressure groups in other countries and regions to conform to the new international order. An example of such nongovernmental pressures is the cutoff by international banks of low interest loans to South Africa, among other sanctions, to force democratic elections—elections that ultimately did take place in April 1994. (South Africa also gained international legitimacy by crafting a constitution that is heavily infused with the idiom of international human rights principles and law.) Global interdependence makes the Euro-Atlantic community's linkage of human rights and foreign relations all the more consequential.

Thus an old faultline between the Euro-Atlantic core and the "Third World" is broken anew—all the more so as the Euro-Atlantic community and institutions push to extend human rights governance. Ironically, in the face of such pressures, Westphalian incantations of sovereignty are heard today no more loudly than in the Third World.[57] "We recognize," the OSCE states declared in the Charter of Paris, "the essential contribution of our common European culture and our shared values in overcoming the division of the continent."[58] In creating a transatlantic community, global political and culture fissures are brought, once more, to the surface.

7

Nations without States

REFLECTIONS ON A CHANGING
LANDSCAPE

We live in a world where the "neighborhood" has been rendered prob-
lematical. For many Turks in Germany and Mexicans in the United States,
home, in the metaphoric as well as in the literal sense, is somewhere else.
Even "nationals," classically understood, increasingly fear that they will
become foreigners in their own countries as the cultural, ethnic, and
religious hues of "their homeland" become ever more nuanced.[1] Living in
a diaspora is becoming the common experience. Similarly, domestic
society has become a microcosm of the world at large: North-South
divisions have been domesticated. At the crux of this development is a
progressive breakdown of the notion that political identity and, hence,
political agency are functions of the sovereign control of a territory.[2]

The splitting of "the nation" from the territorial state exclusive to one
group, hints at—indeed anticipates—the delinking of social, cultural, and
even national self-determination from territoriality. The fading of the
unitarist nation-state exacts a heavy price, as is evident in the growing
civil and ethnic dissension in Western Europe and in the United States. As
these societies lose their taken-for-granted assumptions, rooted in a hitherto collective conscience, civil life in general is corroded.[3] Yet the
deterritorialization of political life holds out a promise too. The multiplic-
ity of ethnic groups and the absence of contiguity of such groups make
any notion of territorially based self-determination patently impossible.[4]
However, insofar as such groups can make claims on states on the basis of
international human rights law and, hence, become recognized actors in
the international arena, territoriality becomes less critical to self-determination. An important caveat, however, is that these developments are not

universal and are limited to Western Europe and North America. Clearly we are witnessing the opposite tendency in Eastern Europe—namely, the territorialization of communal identity.

If the feudal arrangement of political and social space can be conceived of as hierarchical and centripetal, the nation-state has been projected as horizontal and boundary oriented. The feudal and dynastic regimes stressed an axial and sacred center blessed, as it were, by divine intervention, and mediating between heaven and earth. Borders were porous and undefined. The modern state was, in contrast, flat, homogeneous, and carefully mapped, but the Land and the People, irrevocably tied to one another, were sacralized.[5]

In the process of territorialization that formally began with the emergence of the nation-state, three concepts of "bounded space" were superimposed on one another: the notions of community, polity, and territory became so interlinked that the distinctions ceased to be apparent to the average citizen. A brief examination of the process of territorialization is appropriate, not to suggest any inevitability in the evolution of historical change, but rather to elucidate how such concepts of social, political, and territorial space are being "unpacked" through the deterritorialization of communal identity that is now occurring.

Nation-states, writes Benedict Anderson, were conceded to be "new," but the nations to which they gave expression came out of an immemorial past and reached into an endless and golden future. Nationalist imaginings had a strong affinity with religious imaginings.[6] Indeed, nations were first imagined in religious terms.

This chapter reflects on the emergence and implications of a deterritorialized identity. A consideration how historically nation, state, and territoriality became fused is followed by an analysis of how transnational migration is leading to the separation of "nation" and (territorial) state. The emerging forms of community, polity, and territoriality will then be explored, with a brief discussion of the risks and promises inherent in these changes.

The Territorialization of Faith

Certain crucial events summarize antecedent processes and frame the direction of future developments.[7] The Peace of Westphalia of 1648 is one such crucial event, in particular the principle enunciated then: *cuius regio, eius religio.* That principle recognized the *territorial* deadlock that had resulted from the struggle between Catholics and Protestants; but in many respects it reflected a Protestant concept of separate peoples, tied to distinct churches, associated with specific lands. Although this nationalist concept was later to be secularized, let us not forget the importance of institutionalized faiths in nationalist struggles, from the Dutch Reformed Church in both the Netherlands and South Africa to the Church of England.[8] God, after all, was an Englishman and the Puritans in America were the New Israel. In *cuius regio, eius religio*, territory (*regio*), a "people" (initially identified with its church), and, through the stress on independence, the polity were apparently inextricably linked.

The Protestant Reformation both "flattened" the medieval church and delimited it; that is, Protestantism set up the framework for a horizontal and boundary-oriented entity.[9] Rejecting the role of the medieval church in mediating salvation and in regulating social relations more generally, the Protestants emphasized the individual and collective sharing of grace in place of the hierarchic distribution of grace in the Catholic Church.[10] Through this process, the universality of the church was dissolved. The hierarchical conception of society was undermined. In its place, diversity and equality became the rule within the bounds of Christendom. The band of saints, the collectivity, imbued with the grace of God, became the sovereign people: absolute political authority would rest in the community.[11] Equally important, the term *self-determination* took on a social and political resonance. The idea of self-determination was the converse of church mediation: it reflected the aspiration to determine one's own destiny, and not to be ruled by others. (According to the *Oxford English Dictionary* the use of the word self as a prefix, as in "self-determination" or in "self-realization," first appears in English in the sixteenth century, and multiplies rapidly in use in the seventeenth century. Self-determination as a specific term first appears in the seventeenth century.)

The "territorialization of faiths," to use Anderson's term, was not only a structural outcome of the struggle for the soul of Christendom. Territorialism was inherent in the Protestant missions, at least among the Protestant churches and denominations, such as the different Calvinist groups, the Lutherans, and the Anglicans, that concerned themselves with the establishment of autonomous states. The Church of Rome saw ecclesiastical and temporal authority as distinct realms. Catholicism was otherworldly, monastic in its ideals. This world, this earth, this *territory* was to be "escaped."

The initial Protestant impulse was otherworldly and apolitical (most notably among the Anabaptists and the Millenarians), but in seeking to escape the "earthly kingdom" they created a crisis of order: Who was to defend the new faith against the armies of Rome seeking to extirpate this heresy? The Protestant churches that followed, on the other hand, sought to transform politics into a calling (the "saint" anticipating the citizen), to bring about the Kingdom of God on earth.[12] The temporal became the measure of progress toward salvation, toward the eschaton. "To the Protestant," H. Richard Niebuhr wrote, ". . . life seems a pilgrim's progress which, whether made in solitary or in company, proceeds through unpredictability and crises toward the destination beyond life and death where all trumpets blow."[13] The linearity of time, stressing a sacred past and a heavenly future in contrast to static medieval conceptions, preceded and nurtured historical conceptions of nations and nationhood. The nation—nationalism—sought, like Protestantism, a way *into* history, to give soteriological meaning to temporal existence, *to conquer and to transform this world, this earth, this territory.*[14]

Community (be it Dutch, English, or American, for example), polity (such as consociational, parliamentarian, or constitutional) and territory became a sacralized and single entity. Not only were these communities nationally "imagined," in that members never knew personally their fellow members, but they had a "global imagination" as well: the national community belonged to a "family of (like-minded) nations." The boundaries of each nation were set off by other nations. The family of nations concept, truly global in its reach, had its Christian and Western European precursor. As one Calvinist people, the Afrikaners, expressed it over a hundred years ago: "[We] are a Christian people . . . part of the great community of nations who all participate in Christian civilization, and between whose members fraternal relations exist which could not [be arrived at] between Israel and other peoples."[15] Prior to the Reformation, in contrast, the "borders" of the church were indistinct and in principle unlimited and, furthermore, on a distinctly different level from those of community. Social horizons generally did not extend beyond the family, manor, or shire. Political relations were based on family and private treaty, and were patriarchal and affective.[16] Little concern was devoted to "borders" as such.

Post-Westphalia Europe is characterized chiefly (but not wholly) by absolutist rulers claiming divine sanction rather than popular support. Still, the framework set up by Westphalia encouraged attempts of rulers to "unmake" the myriad feudal distinctions and, in its place, fashion a unified and homogeneous state. Politics, as a consequence, became increasingly "public" and "national," as well as class based, as the rulers sought the resources and support of their countries (and, in particular, of the emergent bourgeoisie) in interstate conflicts.[17] Territoriality, even under dynastic rule, had an incipient nationalist flavor. The parallel in this respect between dynastic and nationalist rule is captured in the words of Shakespeare, writing at the end of the sixteenth century in the reign of the zealously Protestant Queen Elizabeth I:

> This royal throne of kings, this scepter'd isle
> This earth of majesty, this seat of Mars,
> This other Eden, demi-paradise . . .
> This happy breed of men, this little world;
> This precious stone set in the silver sea . . .
> *This blessed plot, this earth, this realm, this England* . . .[18]

By the late nineteenth century the states system had through Western conquest and colonization become a global phenomenon. By fiat, Western forms of political organization became the predominant model. The states system was secularized, and non-Christian states (like Turkey) were formally recognized as sovereign states. The dynamic behind secularization—rationalism—acted to reinforce, however, premises that had taken root at Westphalia; rationalism stressed the idea of the citizen and the individual who called the state his or her home, the system of uniform law, the idea of legal equality, the idea of the state that exists to serve its citizens. It further legitimized, too, the idea of loyalty to a group larger than the clan or the manor.[19] Rationalism, however, did not undo the sacred quality of the nation. The transcendent and soteriological promise of religion was nationalized. Millions would march to their deaths for their country and would be immortalized in their nation's history.[20]

New Frontiers

"The manifestation of the sacred," Mircea Eliade wrote, "founds the world." The sacred makes orientation possible; it founds the world in that it defines space, limits, and boundaries and it thus establishes the order of the world. Space is organized through delimiting the sacred; the homogeneity of space is broken by the sacred. In traditional societies the sacred is the center of the world, the *axis-mundi*, where heaven and earth meet. All ritual is directed toward that center, which can be a Holy Land (such as Israel), a city (Jerusalem or Mecca), or a sanctuary (the Temple Mount). The profane, conversely, represents the unformed. Settling a territory is equivalent to founding a new world. The symbolism of the center is the formative principle in the creation of cities, temples, and simple dwellings. When, for example, the Spanish and Portuguese conquistadors conquered territories in the name of Christianity, what was profane territory, and hence identified with chaos, became sacralized, symbolically *ordered* and oriented, by the raising of the cross. To settle, to inhabit a place, is to replicate the cosmogony and to do the work of the gods.[21]

Likewise, the nation-state even in its most secularized form, is not only imagined but is a unit of being, a way of founding the world, a mode of orientation to the world. The nation is the primordial center, the ultimate point of reference, for its members.[22]

In being boundary oriented, the (nation)-state depends on those boundaries being effectively maintained. The entry of undocumented or illegal immigrants, or the settlement of guest workers, is not simply a violation of the law of the recipient country. It is a violation of sacred space and of a primordial category. This, in the main, is why in the United States and Western Europe the issue of illegal immigrants and guest workers has raised concern, passion, and conflict.[23] Given the interwoven character of territory, polity, and community in the nation-state, migrants cannot be viewed as, say, harmless transients (as passersby could be so construed in the Middle Ages); they become a threat to the boundaries of the (national) community as well. Thus immigrants and other foreign influences are sometimes viewed as "corrupting" and "polluting" the body politic.

A bounded territory is not so much *the* defining characteristic of the nation-state as it is a precondition for demarcating the boundaries of a national community. In the nation-state the process of self-determination is inextricable from the drawing of boundaries and of borders. Where community and territory are fused, the breaching of territorial boundaries does not only threaten the integrity of the national community; *the territory itself is desacralized.*

The progressive desacralization of territory does not mean that borders have been erased; all kinds of borders designating all kinds of entities exist. We have borders that delineate provinces, states in the United States, regional borders that encompass, for example, the European Union; we even have borders that intersect in patchwork-like fashion, such as those of the European Union (EU), the Organization for Security and Cooperation in Europe (OSCE), and the member states of the European Convention on Human Rights (ECHR). Borders as such do not denote any sacredness—the borders of Arizona, for example, do not take on any soteriological significance for its residents, whereas Arizonans have sacrificed their lives for the United States. Thus while national borders continue to exist, their "interiors" increasingly take on a more mundane significance in the Euro-Atlantic community. The patchwork, intersecting boundaries that we observe in Europe today are in part an expression of that desacralization—borders, in becoming less sacrosanct, can be "crossed," superseded, and complemented by other kinds of authorities (and *their* boundary markers). Just as important, the state itself can be reconfigured as an instrument for a broader international order. In this limited respect, Western Europe of today reflects medieval Europe. Feudalism also had its "patchwork of overlapping and incomplete rights of government," which were "inextricably . . . tangled," and in which "different juridical instances were geographically interwoven and stratified, and plural allegiances . . . abounded."[24]

The desacralization of territory and the fraying of national communal boundaries produces, however, a precarious condition for the social and political order. In a desacralized world no point of reference can be established and no orientation to the world is revealed. A statement of Mircea Eliade written over thirty-five years ago exquisitely, if unwittingly, captures the postmodern condition:

> The profane experience . . . maintains the homogeneity and hence the relativity of space. No *true* orientation is now possible, for the fixed point no longer enjoys a unique ontological status; it appears and disappears in accordance with the needs of the day. Properly speaking, there is no longer any world, there are only fragments of a shattered universe, an amorphous mass consisting of an infinite number of more or less neutral places in which man moves, governed by the obligations of an existence incorporated into an industrial society. (emphasis in original)[25]

If the sacred makes orientation possible in that it defines space, limits, and boundaries—in this case, the boundaries of state and nation—then desacralization brings the boundaries of the national community into question. If the nation-state is in the process of being desacralized, what other social, communal, and political forms are coming to the fore?

New Expanses

Under the impact of the transnational movement of people, and its reforming of the way social and political community is constituted, the nation-state is being "unpacked." Community, polity, and territory are becoming separate and distinct entities or spheres: the (territorial) state, if present trends continue, is in the process of becoming a territorial administrative unit of a supranational legal and political order based on human rights. The polity is in the process of being transposed to a transnational level as an entity based on human rights codes (namely the Euro-Atlantic community) and the state the institutional forum—the territorial locus—of that legal-political order. That does not signify the emergence of a "super state"—the present states, for example, retain control over military power. Nor is this international legal and political order an object of allegiance in any "globalistic" sense—it does *not* indicate the emergence of a "global community." Rather, the state's purposes now become inclusive rather than exclusive or enclosed. The state's purpose is now to defend and advance this larger community in which it is now legally embedded.

Communal boundaries are of another order. The "imagined community" of the nation-state was bounded, finite, and internally characterized by a deep, uniform, and horizontal comradeship. Other nations, beyond its borders, belonged to the "foreign" or the "alien."[26] In the emerging order, we still have imagined communities—be they ethnic, religious, or in other forms—but instead of being horizontal, territorial, and boundary oriented they are transterritorial and centripetal. Boundaries are *culturally* (rather than politically or physically) meaningful. Because the "imagination" is not a territorial one, communities can be juxtaposed; communal space is truly imagined and thus not constrained, in principle, by other communities so organized. Communities are both local and removed, subnational and transterritorial. The neighborhood is transnational and "the world" lives in the neighborhood. The symbolic center for many is not the place of their residence but elsewhere; a world is founded in Eliade's terms, but "we" live in the diaspora. Illustrative of this detached quality, as it were, is the very low propensity of permanent residents who were formerly migrants to seek naturalization in both the United States and Western Europe (see chaps. 2 and 3). Such developments do not indicate the emergence of a global community; in fact social distinctions are becoming ever more multifarious. In the deterritorialization of identity, communities can live together but in different "worlds." (Ethnic neighborhoods are no longer picturesque spots in an otherwise homogeneous landscape, but "exclaves" with transnational ties.) Eliade, referring to a different context but one equally applicable for the emerging global condition, noted:

> The multiplicity, or even the infinity, of centers of the world raises no difficulty for religious [or communal] thought. For it is not a matter of geometrical space, but of an existential and sacred space that has entirely different structure, that admits of an infinite number of breaks, and hence is capable of an infinite number of communications.[27]

As Habermas puts it, one's "own national tradition will, in each case, have to be appropriated in such a manner that it is related to and relativized by the vantage points of other national cultures."[28]

The centripetal element of transterritorial communities is that they are symbolically "centered." A sacred center "ontologically founds the world"; it is a marker for ethnic, religious, or cultural groups. Like the nation, a sacred and mythic center conjures up the image of a people with cosmic beginnings and a golden future. The center, the *axis-mundi*, shifts: Africa for many African-Americans (the change from the description "black Americans" is significant here), Israel for many Jews, Aztlan for Chicano groups, and the traditional sacred centers for, say, Muslims in Europe or American Indians, to name just a few examples.

Unlike the nation-state, actual residence in the center is not critical to "belonging." Communities can, consequently, live in the same locations in a patchwork fashion—the uniformity of the nation-state is not necessarily aspired to.

For many the mythic promise of the nation will hold true but the nation will be "compartmentalized." In everyday life, the imagined community will cease to be shared and homogeneous. Instead, increasingly there will be imagined communit*ies*, sometimes intersecting, sometimes not. Depending on the context, the individual may even be able to "switch imaginations"—a Muslim Turk living in Germany, for example, may have multiple points of reference.

New Civilities

Associations of various kinds—religious, ethnic, social, economic, and so on—have always existed. In terms of the classic image of the nation-state, the sovereign state was the one compulsory association. As such it was the only political association formally recognized on the global stage. An individual or, say, an ethnic association could be recognized in the international arena only insofar as it had a state as its representative. In the light of the changes described in this book, in particular the ability of nonstate entities to make claims on the state (theirs or others in the Euro-Atlantic community), such nonstate groups become international actors in their own right.

The bifurcation of the "nation" from the territorial state poses certain risks. Once the stress on the notion of the state as a entity that transcends all internal ethnic, religious, class, and political differences, of the state as the one compulsory association that unites all the people in its territory in a common national identity—once this stress is lost, we risk subnational divisions along, for example, ethnic lines. On the other hand, the increasing ability of groups to be recognized outside territorial frameworks may be seen as holding out a promise for a civil political life.

The opportunity lies in the gradual stripping of the state as *the* actor in international relations. The state's role as the organizing principle in international relations has meant that all problems and grievances had to be solved through the framework of the state; many groups, however, are not fully represented by the state and, most important, many groups are not recognized by it. They cannot practice "self-determination" or become "a part of history" unless they are territorially based sovereign entities.

The ability of groups to seek redress of grievances on the basis of international law and institutions (through national forums or regional and international forums like the OSCE and the ECHR) may become one critical mechanism in resolving conflict. The other, equally critical, possibility is that through giving nonstate groups *recognition* as nonterritorial actors in the international arena they can become "a part of history" and "determine their own destiny." Recognition, in this context, has an ontological as well as a political importance. Similarly, as the state is gradually transformed into a forum for a wider international and constitutional framework, so its appeal as a means of national self-definition will lessen, at least in the Euro-Atlantic core.[29]

Such an international constitutional order based on human rights, centered in the Euro-Atlantic community, appears to reflect present trends in international law. That, of course, does not mean that the trend is irreversible. Creating "a condition of peace" requires policy to reflect present trends in international law and to reinforce those trends by, for example, strengthening nonstate actors' ability to make claims on states on the basis of international law. It also means making nonstate actors more accountable for their actions under international law (such as terrorist, guerrilla, and militia groups that violate human rights norms) and bringing them under international censure.

Enforcement mechanisms, in the form of intervention and collective security, must be brought to bear on all parties, state or nonstate, in order to uphold the international human rights order.

The growing literature on collective security fails, Richard Betts notes, to address the sociological and political basis necessary for collective security. As Betts puts it, collective security demands an extraordinary change in the character of the states system; a "community of power" concept is necessary to replace the "balance of power" concept, which has been the imputed basis of international security at least until recently.[30] With the state's very judicial and jurisdictional existence predicated on a broader constitutional order based on human rights, the state becomes a part of a broader community (represented by institutions like the OSCE). Thus such a security regime has a sociological and political framework that makes collective security a real possibility.[31]

Similarly there is a great degree of confusion about when intervention is permissible or desirable. The oft used standard of "national interest" in media reports, op-ed columns, and academic debate stems from a more traditional understanding of international relations and of intervention. By contrast, human rights norms are now beginning to become a basis for intervention, as noted in chapter 6, as is evident in Haiti and Somalia, in the negotiations between former Yugoslavia parties and Western countries, and, over a longer period, in foreign aid appropriations.[32]

Even if the legal framework is clarified, the *specific* measures taken in a given crisis will not be self-evident. Consideration whether military intervention, for example, should be undertaken in a given circumstance will involve a variety of tactical, logistical, and other concerns. But the overarching framework will legitimate intervention when human rights norms are being violated and that in itself will force states *and* nonstate parties to act with this in mind, or risk the consequences. For all the birth pangs associated with this new principle in Bosnia and in Somalia, there can be little doubt that the right of intervention on humanitarian and human rights grounds is here to stay.

What is also clear is that we have to rethink our theoretical approaches to explaining "how the world works." Prevalent theoretical approaches in international relations and political sociology to the state cannot readily account for the changes described in this book. Neorealists and structuralists rarely, if ever, understood the state as socially constituted and, consequently, as a potentially problematic entity. Nor did (or do) such theorists consider how contemporary social, political, and economic forces may be "reconstituting" the state, let alone consider the impact of immigration. In the world according to neorealism, the cross-national flow of people could be controlled or reversed if it was in the interests of the state to do so. As observed in this book, states have sought to control transnational immigration and, in the 1970s and 1980s, they failed.

Similarly, the belief of such theorists that the state is a self-evident and "natural" phenomenon, a there-for-all-to-see bureaucratic and territorial entity, means that more nuanced contemporary developments are, analytically speaking, out of the picture. They are seemingly compelled to explain away the evident and growing importance of transnational human rights in legitimating states. How, given structuralist and neorealist assumptions, could the state's legitimacy be increasingly rooted in a transnational order? How could a state be "constituted"? Instead, to explain a clearly changing world, such scholars turn to circumlocutions like "pooled sovereignties." In this way the state always *is*; it is never reconstituted. The state just changes its tactics.

Poststructuralism fares better in that such an approach does consider how social, political, and economic challenges, including immigration, implicate how the state is "constructed." However, poststructuralists, drawn by a philosophical commitment to deconstruction, have difficulties understanding that (state) authority is being recentered in human rights. Poststructuralists may be drawn to, say, Bosnia, as an example of postmodernism, but they apparently have difficulty in understanding the local and worldwide aversion to that existence. The question that poststructuralists exclude out of hand is, What organizing principle or principles are emerging to order the world? This study clearly points to the growing importance of human rights in that respect.

"I want to reach that state of condensation of sensations," the artist Henri Matisse reportedly once said, "which constitutes a picture." We may have enough pixels, or "sensations," to capture the outlines of a picture—a picture still developing, so to speak. Many questions remain, however. What do the developments discussed in this book suggest for the shape and form of domestic politics?[33] How are the markers of ethnic, religious, and other groups constituted? In what way do such groups come to be represented? What role does the media play?[34] What does the stress on "rights" bode for democracy and the legislative process? *Novus Ordo Seclorum* indeed.

Notes

1 Novus Ordo Seclorum

1. See B. Bouckaert, "Between Freedom and State Sovereignty," *Nederlands Tidschrift voor Rechtsfilosophie en Rechttheoric* 18, 3 (1989): 237–47; Liah Greenfeld, *Nationalism: Five Roads to Modernity* (Cambridge, Mass.: Harvard University Press, 1992), 10; and Allan Rosas, "Democracy and Human Rights," in Allan Rosas and Jan Helgesen, eds., *Human Rights in a Changing East-West Perspective* (London: Pinter, 1990), 18–23. Until recently at least, the state, not the individual, has been the object of international law (see chaps. 4 and 5). After the Peace of Westphalia in 1648, in which the system of states is conventionally viewed as having its beginnings, the state was now expected under international law to respect basic "natural rights" of its people. See John S. Gibson, *International Organizations, Constitutional Law and Human Rights* (New York: Praeger, 1991), 139–40.
2. Bouckaert, "Between Freedom and State Sovereignty," 237, and Louis Henkin, *The Age of Rights* (New York: Columbia University Press, 1990), 144.
3. Challenges as to the "universality" of human rights were mounted at the international conference on human rights in Vienna, 1993, by some Third World countries. This reflects, more than anything, global fissures concerning the criteria of state legitimacy with—ironically, given the Western roots of the concept—many Third World countries maintaining the principle of sovereignty. This will be discussed further in chap. 6.
4. The Hegelian usage of the term *Aufhebung*, as described by Shlomo Avineri, resonates here. *Aufhebung* captures the dialectic of abolition, transcendence, and preservation. International human rights abolishes and transcends the nation-state and yet it preserves critical elements of it on a "higher" plane. See Avineri, *The Social and Political Thought of Karl Marx* (Cambridge: Cambridge University Press, 1971), 37.
5. Similarly, nationalism is often viewed as dividing, if not divisive, with its more virulent strains being mistaken as the norm. However, as Hans Kohn pointed out,

nationalism has not only prepared the ground for "mass participation" in politics, but has brought about contact between different peoples and civilizations. In this way, even nationalism contributed to the idea of universal values. See *The Idea of Nationalism* (New York: Macmillan, 1944).

6. Even under the absolutist rulers, a certain incipient "nationalism" was evident. This is discussed further in chap. 2 and in the conclusion.

7. See Harold Laski, *Foundations of Sovereignty* (Freeport, N.Y.: Books for Libraries Press, 1968 [1921]), 1–29; and F. H. Hinsley, *Sovereignty* (London: Watts, 1966).

8. Cynthia Weber, "Reconsidering Statehood: Examining the Sovereignty/Intervention Boundary," *Review of International Studies* 18 (1992): 199–216.

9. Legitimacy is "that quality of rule which derives from a perception on the part of those to whom it is addressed that it has come into being in accordance with the right process." See Thomas M. Franck, "Legitimacy in the International System," *American Journal of International Law* 82 (1988): 706.

10. The stress on territoriality has gone hand in hand with a conception of the state as a bureaucratic entity with sovereign control over a fixed territory. See Kenneth Waltz, *Theory of International Politics* (Reading, Mass.: Addison-Wesley, 1979), and Gianfranco Poggi, *The Development of the Modern State: A Sociological Introduction* (Stanford: Stanford University Press, 1978). Territoriality is not a concern as such of Waltz but the state is projected as a unitary actor that is, implicitly, territorially bounded. Poggi sees the emergence of the modern state as beginning with the "strengthening of territorial rule and the absorption of smaller and weaker territories into larger and stronger ones [which] led to the formation of a relatively small number of mutually independent states, each defining itself as sovereign and engaged with others in an inherently open-ended, competitive, and risk-laden power struggle" (60).

11. A territory can have, of course, sacred and mythic importance for a people, as is the case for almost any national movement. But this illustrates the sociological (rather than the territorial) axis of the nation-state. The Zionist movement, for example, refused British offers at the turn of the century of the territory of Uganda: the aim was not simply to establish a (territorial) state where any piece of real estate would do, but to establish a new nation in the ancestral Land of Israel. The Land of Israel was critical because it had sacred connotations for, and ties to, the People of Israel, the Jews.

12. Rogers Brubaker, *Citizenship and Nationhood in France and Germany* (Cambridge, Mass.: Harvard University Press, 1992), 22–23.

13. See Ruth Lapidoth, "Sovereignty in Transition," *Journal of International Affairs* 45, 2 (1992): 330. On nonintervention, see UNGA Resolution 2625 (XXV), cited in Lapidoth. The principle of nonintervention is eroding under the impact of international human rights law, which will be discussed in chap. 6.

14. John Gerard Ruggie, "Territoriality and Beyond: Problematizing Modernity in International Relations," *International Organization* 47, 1 (1993): 140.

15. The assumption is, at least in the neorealist tradition, that states in one form or another have existed since time immemorial; states, so to speak, "preexist." (I am grateful to Richard Ashley for this point.) Yet migrations have been at the root of, for example, the formation of world empires. A recent attempt to draw interna-

tional relations theory into discussions on immigration is James Hollifield, *Immigrants, Markets and States: The Political Economy of Postwar Europe* (Cambridge, Mass.: Harvard University Press, 1992). Recent work by sociologists who have considered the ramifications of transnational migration on the nation-state are referenced in chap. 2.

16. Michael Walzer, *Spheres of Justice: A Defense of Pluralism and Equality* (New York: Basic Books, 1983), 62.

17. Weber, "Reconsidering Statehood," 215–16.

18. Jürgen Habermas, "Citizenship and National Identity: Some Reflections on the Future of Europe," *Praxis International* 12, 1 (1992): 16.

19. See Robert Reich, *The Work of Nations* (New York: Alfred A. Knopf, 1991). On the impact of different kinds of transnational activities on the state, see David Jacobson, "A Nation's Sovereignty under Siege: The United States in an Age of Global Interdependence," (Ph.D. diss., Princeton University, 1991).

20. One could argue that in human life "movement" and social and political "space" are as intricately related as "space" and "time" are in the physical sciences. That the global movement of people shifted from South to North in the 1950s, that Communist countries contained the movement of their people, that freedom in Eastern Europe created a flood of immigrants, that new migratory patterns developed in the 1980s with new destinations such as Japan—all these developments have, it hardly has to be said, larger social and political implications. See Department of Economic and Social Development, *Report on the World Social Situation* (New York: United Nations, 1993), 14–17.

21. Hollifield, *Immigrants, Markets, and States*, 232.

22. An interesting exception is South Africa, admittedly always difficult to classify in terms of the North-South distinction. The idiom of human rights in its political discourse and its new constitution, as well as the use of international observers in the April 1994 elections, illustrates the degree to which human rights have become an essential means to international legitimacy.

23. See Brubaker, *Citizenship and Nationhood in Germany*, 35.

24. Habermas, "Citizenship and National Identity," 12. As Habermas puts it, citizenship "is an answer to the [question] 'Who am I?'" (16).

25. Maxim Silverman, "Citizenship and the Nation State in France," *Ethnic and Racial Studies* 14, 3 (1991): 333.

26. See Peter Schuck and Rogers M. Smith, *Citizenship without Consent* (New Haven: Yale University Press, 1985).

27. See the introduction to William Rogers Brubaker, ed., *Immigration and the Politics of Citizenship in Europe and North America* (Lanham, Md.: University Press of America, 1989), 1–13.

28. See Martin Heisler, "Transnational Migration as a Small Window on the Diminished Autonomy of the Modern Democratic State," *Annals* (AAPSS) 485, (May 1986): 153–66.

29. Waltz, *Theory of International Politics*.

30. See Theda Skocpol, *States and Social Revolutions* (Cambridge: Cambridge University Press, 1979); and Poggi, *The Development of the Modern State*.

31. George M. Thomas and John W. Meyer, "The Expansion of the State," *Annual Review of Sociology* 10 (1984): 461–82.
32. Ruggie, "Territoriality and Beyond," 139–40.
33. John Meyer, "The World Polity and the Authority of the Nation-State," in George M. Thomas, John Meyer, Francisco Ramirez, and John Boli, *Institutional Structure: Constituting State, Society and the Individual* (Beverly Hills, Calif.: Sage, 1987), 41–70; and Martin Wight, *Systems of States* (Leceister: Leceister University Press, 1977), 113–14.
34. See Bertrand Badie and Pierre Birnbaum *The Sociology of the State* (Chicago: University of Chicago Press, 1983).
35. Thomas and Meyer, "The Expansion of the State," 463; they cite Badie and Birnbaum, *The Sociology of the State*.
36. Ernst-Otto Czempiel and James Rosenau, *Global Changes and Theoretical Challenges* (Lexington, Mass., Lexington Books, 1989); and James der Derian, *International/Intertextual Relations* (Lexington, Mass.: Lexington Books, 1989).
37. See essays in Stephen Krasner, ed., *International Regimes* (Ithaca: Cornell University Press, 1983).
38. Alex Wendt, "The Agent-Structure Problem in International Theory," *International Organization* 41, 3 (1987): 335–70.
39. See, for example, essays in Thomas et al., *Institutional Structure*.
40. John Boli, "Human Rights or State Expansion? Cross-National Definitions of Constitutional Rights, 1870–1970," in Thomas et al., *Institutional Structure*, 133–49.
41. Within the Stanford approach some promising work has recently been undertaken that considers notions of "global culture" and of a transnational order. See, for example, John Boli and George Thomas, "International Non-Governmental Organizations in the World Polity" (Department of Sociology, Arizona State University, 1994, manuscript).
42. Martin Shapiro and Alec Stone, "The New Constitutional Politics of Europe," *Comparative Political Studies* 26, 4 (1994): 397–420.
43. Although for the sake of simplicity the term *state* is used generically, the discussion pertains to the states in the Euro-Atlantic core of the international order.
44. Shapiro and Stone, noting the scarcity of research on the judiciary in contrast to the extensive studies of the legislature, political parties, and the like, attribute it first, to the strong commitment to the separation of law and politics, and second, to the interdisciplinary approach to the study of the law and the courts that would be required for political scientists. See "The New Constitutional Politics of Europe," 397–98.
45. Joseph R. Strayer, *On the Medieval Origins of the Modern State* (Princeton: Princeton University Press, 1970).
46. See David Jacobson and George M. Thomas, "The Growth of Global Judicial Authority through Human Rights Instruments" (Department of Sociology, Arizona State University, 1994, manuscript); Perry Anderson, *Lineages of the Absolutist State* (London: Verso, 1974); Pierre Birnbaum, "State, Centre and Bureaucracy," *Government and Opposition*, 16 (1981): 58–77; and Poggi, *The Development of the Modern State*.

47. R. Bendix, *Nation Building and Citizenship* (New York: Wiley, 1964), and T. H. Marshall, *Citizenship and Social Class* (New York: Doubleday, 1948).

48. Boli, "Human Rights or State Expansion?"

49. Marshall, *Citizenship and Social Class*; Bendix, *Nation Building and Citizenship*; and Boli, "Human Rights or State Expansion?"

50. A distinction has to be drawn between migrants and refugees. Here the focus is on the former group. The problems associated with each group are not necessarily the same. Migrant populations, as an aggregate, *generally* have longer and deeper associations with their host countries and their movements are a function, in part at least, of market conditions. Refugees are a product of forced relocation, or are fearful for their physical well-being or are fleeing political, ethnic, or religious persecution. An extensive literature is available on refugee issues and international law. See, for example, Maryellen Fullerton, "The International and National Protection of Refugees," in Hurst Hannum, ed., *Guide to International Human Rights Practice*, 2d ed. (Philadelphia: University of Pennsylvania Press, 1992), 211–27.

2   Immigration and Citizenship in Western Europe

1. Joseph R. Strayer, *On the Medieval Origins of the Modern State* (Princeton: Princeton University Press, 1970).

2. Donald W. Hanson, *From Kingdom to Commonwealth* (Cambridge, Mass.: Harvard University Press, 1970), 15–20, 340–43, and Michael Walzer, *The Revolution of the Saints* (Cambridge, Mass.: Harvard University Press, 1965), 4–10; Walzer cites Daniel Lerner, *The Passing of Traditional Society* (New York: Free Press of Glencoe, 1958). See also Marc Bloch, *Feudal Society*, trans. L. A. Manyon (Chicago: University of Chicago Press, 1961).

3. See Garrett Mattingly, *Renaissance Diplomacy* (London: Jonathan Cape, 1955).

4. Hanson, *From Kingdom to Commonwealth*, 340–41.

5. Rogers Brubaker, *Citizenship and Nationhood in France and Germany* (Cambridge, Mass.: Harvard University Press, 1992), 25.

6. The phrase is taken from Benedict Anderson, *Imagined Communities: Reflections on the Origins and Spread of Nationalism* (London: Verso, 1983).

7. See Gianfranco Poggi, *The Development of the Modern State: A Sociological Introduction* (Stanford: Stanford University Press, 1978), 60–65.

8. Aristide R. Zolberg, "Contemporary Transnational Migrations in Historical Perspective," in M. Kritz, ed., *U.S. Immigration and Refugee Policy* (Lexington, Mass.: Lexington Books, 1983), 20. Zolberg cites D. B. Glass, *Population Movements in Europe* (London: Frank Cass, 1967), 91.

9. Zolberg, "Contemporary Transnational Migrations in Historical Perspective," 21.

10. A. W. Orridge, "Varieties of Nationalism," in Leonard Tivey, ed., *The Nation State: The Formation of Modern Politics* (New York: St. Martin's, 1981), 42.

11. Martin Wight, *Systems of States* (Leicester: Leicester University Press, 1977), 113–14.

12. W. R. Böhning, "International Migration in the Western World," *International Migration* 16 (1978): 13, and Tomas Hammar, "Citizenship: Membership of a Nation and of a State," *International Migration* 24 (1986): 736.

13. Hammar, "Citizenship," 736–37. About half a million foreigners lived in France in the mid-nineteenth century, 250,000 in Belgium, and 100,000 in the Netherlands. See H. Werner, "Post-War Labour Migration in Western Europe," *International Migration* 24 (1986): 543. See also Zig Layton-Henry, "The Challenge of Political Rights," in Zig Layton-Henry, ed., *The Political Rights of Migrant Workers in Western Europe* (London: Sage, 1990), 1.

14. Tomas Hammar, *Democracy and the Nation State* (Aldershot: Avebury, 1990), 42.

15. See Philip Martin, Elmar Homekopp, and Hans Ullman, "Europe 1992: Effects on Labor Migration," *International Migration Review* 24, 3, (1990): 599–600. In 1987 nearly 5.5 million non-European Community (EC) foreigners resided in Germany and France. Those countries also had (and have) the most EC/EU foreigners—in that year they numbered close to 3 million. In terms of non-EC workers, the two countries accounted for 70 percent of the EC total. The composition of foreigners also shifted dramatically in all European countries from the early 1970s, when most foreigners were from other European countries, through the late 1980s, when the European element of the foreign population was greatly lessened. Europeans constituted over 60 percent of foreigners in France in 1970 but only 37 percent in 1985. The respective figures for Germany were 66 percent in 1974 and 48 percent in 1989. These figures would have clearly been affected by the east-west migrations, particularly from 1989. See figures in Department of Economic and Social Development, *Report on the World Social Situation* (New York: United Nations, 1993), 18.

16. The most recent study is that of Brubaker, *Citizenship and Nationhood in France and Germany*. See also Hans Kohn, *Prelude to Nation-States: The French and German Experience* (Princeton: Van Nostrand, 1967).

17. Anthony D. Smith, *The Ethnic Origins of Nations* (Oxford: Basil Blackwell, 1986), 134–35.

18. Ibid., 137.

19. Brubaker, *Citizenship and Nationhood in France and Germany*, 1–6.

20. Donald L. Horowitz, "Immigration and Group Relations in France and America," in Donald L. Horowitz and Gérard Noiriel, eds., *Immigrants in Two Democracies: French and American Experience* (New York: New York University Press, 1992), 7, 15.

21. See Kohn, *Prelude to Nation-States*, 13–16.

22. Ibid., 16, 21–29.

23. Hammar, "Citizenship," 736.

24. Vida Azimi, "L'étranger sous la Révolution," in *La Révolution et l'ordre juridique privé: Rationalité ou scandale?* (Paris: Presses Universitaires de France, 1988), 702, cited in Brubaker, *Citizenship and Nationhood in France and Germany*, 7.

25. Kohn, *Prelude to Nation-States*, 119–24.

26. Robert M. Berdahl, "New Thoughts on German Nationalism," *American Historical Review* 77 (1972): 66–67. German nationalism, notes Berdahl, was cosmopolitan in that for German nationalists "the nation became the vehicle through which humanity realized its uniqueness and variety, through which it manifested the 'true richness and range of humanity.'"

27. The assimilationist side of French nationhood can be overstated. Zeev Sternhall

notes that since the turn of the century, a more *volkisch* nationalist element, though secondary, has existed in the French body politic, often anti-Semitic and racist. See Sternhall, "The Political Culture of Nationalism," in Robert Tombs, ed., *Nationhood and Nationalism in France: From Boulangism to the Great War, 1889–1918* (New York: Harper Collins, 1991), 22–37. Horowitz and Noiriel note an ethnic element in French national identity going back to the Revolution. See Horowitz, "Immigration and Group Relations," 8.

28. Kohn, *Prelude to Nation-States*, 168–79.

29. Ibid., 168–69. See also Poggi, *The Development of the Modern State*, 74–77.

30. Brubaker, *Citizenship and Nationhood in France and Germany*, 10.

31. Ibid., 16, 25–29.

32. Kay Hailbronner "Citizenship and Nationhood in Germany," in William Rogers Brubaker, ed., *Immigration and Politics of Citizenship in Europe and North America* (Lanham, Md.: University Press of America, 1989), 67.

33. Nora Räthzel, "Germany: One Race, One Nation?" *Race and Class* 32, 3 (1990): 32. German unification in 1989 has raised an interesting debate, with many viewing the unification as the healing of a nation ripped asunder four decades earlier while others, in contrast, see the unification as an opportunity to redefine what is German nationhood (see p. 44).

34. Mark J. Miller, *Foreign Workers in Western Europe* (New York: Praeger, 1981), 7.

35. Tomas Hammar, "Dual Citizenship and Political Integration," *International Migration Review* 19, 3 (1985): 442. Hammar cites OECD, *SOPEMI: Trends in International Migration* (Paris: OECD, 1981) and Hammar's study. Estimating naturalization figures is not unproblematic. See the discussion in Gérard de Rham, "Naturalization: The Politics of Citizenship Acquisition," in Layton Henry, *The Political Rights of Migrant Workers*, 177–83.

36. Figures cited in Brubaker, *Citizenship and Nationhood in France and Germany*, 79–80.

37. A. Perotti, A. Costes and M. Llaumett, "L'Europe et l'immigration," *Migrations Société* 1 (1989): 36; cited in Yasemin Nuhoğlu Soysal, "Limits of Citizenship: Guestworkers in the Contemporary Nation-State System" (Ph.D. diss., Stanford University, 1991), 28. Soysal's dissertation has recently been published in a slightly modified form. See Yasemin Nuhoğlu Soysal, *Limits of Citizenship: Migrants and Postnational Membership in Europe* (Chicago: University of Chicago Press, 1994). All citations that follow refer to the dissertation.

38. Rosemarie Rogers, "The Transnational Nexus of Migration," *Annals* (AAPSS) 485 (May 1986): 40–42, and Soysal, "Limits of Citizenship," 27, 190.

39. Brubaker, *Citizenship and Nationhood in France and Germany*, 80–81.

40. Soysal, "Limits of Citizenship," 46–50, 74–82.

41. See Hammar, "Dual Citizenship."

42. See Jörg Polakiewicz and Valérie Jacob-Foltzer, "The European Human Rights Convention in Domestic Law," *Human Rights Law Journal* 12 (March 28, 1991): 74–81. These topics will be elaborated upon in chap. 4.

43. Georges Tapinos talks of four points at which immigration can be regulated. See "European Migration Patterns Economic Linkages and Policy Experiences," in Kritz, *U.S. Immigration and Refugee Policy*, 64.

44. Western European countries have had an illegal immigration problem but on a much smaller scale than the United States. See statistical estimates and discussion in Catherine Withol de Wenden, "The Absence of Rights: The Position of Illegal Immigrants," in Layton-Henry, *The Political Rights of Migrant Workers*, 27–46.

45. See Soysal, "Limits of Citizenship," 46–50, on German state-society ties. For a different perspective, see James Hollifield's seminal study linking state capacities and markets in the area of immigration: *Immigrants, Markets, and States: The Political Economy of Postwar Europe* (Cambridge, Mass.: Harvard University Press, 1992). Hollifield contrasts the American case, where illegal immigration has been the major factor, to the labor-importing policies of Western European states (pp. 176–79).

46. Hollifield, in *Immigrants, Markets, and States*, 124–40, makes a distinction between state autonomy and state strength. In the case of the French he writes that the state was autonomous enough in the postwar period to pursue a recruitment policy of foreign workers even with opposition from trade unions and some employers. However, France was unable to *implement* the suspension of immigration in 1974. On the failure of immigration suspension policies, see the discussion that follows in this chapter.

47. Illegal aliens in the United States had, as I will discuss in chap. 3, proxy groups to act in their interests, such as agricultural organizations and ethnic groups.

48. See Stephen Castles, *Here for Good: Western Europe's New Ethnic Minorities* (London: Pluto Press, 1987), 11–13.

49. Ibid.

50. Ibid., 11–12.

51. B. Heisler and M. Heisler, "Transnational Migration and the Modern Democratic State," *Annals* (AAPSS) 485 (May 1986): 13.

52. Tapinos, "European Migration Patterns," 56–58.

53. Mark. J. Miller, "Policy Ad-Hocracy: The Paucity of Coordinated Perspectives and Policies," *Annals* (AAPSS) 485 (May 1986): 64–75.

54. Castles, *Here for Good*, 50–51. Castles cites Office National d'Immigration, *Statistiques d'immigration* (Paris, 1968, mimeograph copy).

55. Ibid., 51–53.

56. Ibid, 53–57 (figures cited from OECD, *SOPEMI*, 1982).

57. Ibid, 71–72.

58. James F. Hollifield, "Immigration Policy in France and Germany: Outputs versus Outcomes," *Annals* (AAPSS) 485 (May 1986): 118–19.

59. Castles, *Here for Good*, 71–76.

60. See Werner, "Post-War Labour Migration," 556. In 1982 foreigners constituted 7.6 percent of the population in Germany and 6.8 percent in France. Births among foreigners constituted 11.8 percent and 7.2 percent of total births respectively. However, birthrates of the foreign populations were dropping over time.

61. Aristide Zolberg, "The Next Waves: Migration Theory for a Changing World," *International Migration Review* 23, 2 (1989): 404–5.

62. Myron Weiner, "Immigration: Perspectives from Receiving Countries," *Third World Quarterly* 12, 1 (1990): 140–42.

63. Ibid. See also Vernon Briggs, Jr., *Mass Immigration and the National Interest* (Armonk, N.Y.: M. E. Sharpe, 1992).

64. Hollifield argues, in *Immigration, Markets, and States*, 130, that "the position of workers and employers varied across countries and over time. But, by and large, they have followed their market interests. Major interest groups in the industrial democracies have a stake not only in the formulation of immigration and labor market policy but in the implementation of policy as well. . . . Given this bitter and highly divisive struggle, especially in Western Europe, the position of the state was crucial. Yet the liberal nature of these regimes countered the effective use of a narrow conception of the national interest."

65. Department of Economic and Social Development, *Report*, 16–17.

66. See Alejandro Portes, "International Labor Migration and National Development," in Kritz, *U.S. Immigration and Refugee Policy*, 71.

67. Gary Freeman, "Migration and the Political Economy of the Welfare State," *Annals* (AAPSS) 485 (May 1986): 52–59.

68. Ibid., 55–57.

69. Ibid.

70. Ibid., 53, 58–60.

71. Numerous Mexican migrants were expelled from the United States in the 1950s, a response that would be less tenable today. See chap. 3.

72. Miller, *Foreign Workers in Western Europe*, 84.

73. Jan Vranken, "Industrial Rights," in Layton-Henry, *The Political Rights of Migrant Workers*, 47.

74. Ibid., 47–48, 55.

75. Miller, *Foreign Workers in Western Europe*, 91–95, 110. Only in the 1970s did foreign workers become a significant presence in the unions. In addition to becoming members, the foreign workers were progressively allowed to vote and hold offices in factory councils (Miller, 165). German trade unions are particularly well organized to pressure the political authorities. The French trade union movement is less well situated. By 1980 the rate of unionization of migrants was roughly that of native workers in Germany, whereas in France migrants had a lower rate of unionization than that of French workers. See Vranken, "Industrial Rights," 52–53, 61–63.

76. Miller, *Foreign Workers in Western Europe*, 102, 111, 119–20. See also Vranken, "Industrial Rights," 47.

77. The dual-track strategy by states to control migrants by absorbing those present and creating disincentives for any further migration is a common one—and commonly also fails. See chap. 3 on the American case.

78. J. P. Pilliard, "Patterns and Forms of Immigrant Participation at the Local and National Levels in Western (Continental) Europe," *International Migration* 24 (1986): 508–12, and Uwe Andersen, "Consultative Institutions for Migrant Workers," in Layton-Henry, *The Political Rights of Migrant Workers*, 116–17. The consultative councils have probably been less significant than the other actions and associations of migrants in changing the political landscape of national politics in Western Europe. As Andersen notes, such councils could be used to

justify opposition to granting local voting rights on the basis that the migrants had alternative means of making their voice heard.

79. Miller, *Foreign Workers in Western Europe*, 180–93.
80. Barbara Schmitter, "Immigrants and Associations: Their Role in the Socio-Political Process of Immigrant Worker Integration in West Germany and Switzerland," *International Migration Review* 14, 2 (1980): 184–85.
81. Castles, *Here for Good*, 37–38, and Miller, "Policy Ad-Hocracy," 75.
82. Miller, *Foreign Workers in Western Europe*, 30–68.
83. Ibid., 68, 74–77.
84. Hollifield, "Immigration Policy in France and Germany," 121–23, and Tapinos, "European Migration Patterns," 58.
85. Layton-Henry, "The Challenge of Political Rights," 1.
86. See Yasemin Nuhoğlu Soysal, "Constructions of Immigrant Identities in Europe" (paper presented at the conference on European Identity and Its Intellectual Roots, Cambridge, Massachusetts, May 6–9, 1993).
87. Soysal, "Limits of Citizenship," 174–75, and Tomas Hammar, "The Civil Rights of Aliens," in Layton-Henry, *The Political Rights of Migrant Workers*, 74–93.
88. Soysal, "Limits of Citizenship," 177–79, Brubaker, *Immigration and Politics of Citizenship*, 145–62, and Richard Plender, *International Migration Law* (Dordrecht: Martinus Nijhoff, 1988). The period of stay required for permanent residency status varies from three years in France to eight years in Germany and ten years in Switzerland.
89. Soysal, "Limits of Citizenship," 180–81.
90. Ibid., 179–82, and Jan Rath, "Voting Rights," in Layton-Henry, *The Political Rights of Migrant Workers*, 127–57. It is noteworthy that the Algerian government, among other governments with nationals residing in Europe, has objected to the enfranchisement of their expatriate citizens as a threat to their sovereignty (see Rath, "Voting Rights," 130). Thus transnational migration creates problems of "writing" or defining the nation not only for the receiving countries of migrants but for the sending countries as well.
91. Layton-Henry, "The Challenge of Political Rights," 16.
92. Hammar, *Democracy and the Nation State*, 132.
93. Hammar, "Dual Citizenship and Political Integration," 440–43. Figures for 1980 from OECD, *SOPEMI*, 1981, cited by Hammar. The figures for 1991 range from 5.4 percent in Sweden to 0.2 percent in Belgium. See OECD, *SOPEMI*, 1993, 50.
94. See Hammar, *Democracy and the Nation State*, 84–96.
95. Ibid., 87–88. The 1985 survey, cited by Hammar, is reported in P. König, G. Schultze, and R. Wessel, *Situation de ausländischen Arbeitnehmer und ihrer Familienangehörigen in der Bundesrepublik Deutschland* (Bonn: Forschungsinstitut der Friedrich-Ebert-Stiftung, Der Bundesminister für Arbeit und Sozialordnung, 1986). Hammar writes that no comparable survey data are available on France.
96. See Soysal, "Constructions of Immigrant Identities in Europe."

3   Immigration and Citizenship in the United States

1. F. D. Bean, G. Vernez, and C. B. Kelley, *Opening and Closing the Doors* (Washington, D.C.: Urban Institute, 1989), xv, 1. IRCA pushed the levels of immigration

even higher. In 1989 the number of immigrants, excluding refugees, reached 1.1 million and in 1990 a record high of 1.5 million was registered. See Department of Economic and Social Development, *Report on the World Social Situation* (New York: United Nations, 1993), 16. According to one report, if current trends continue, non-Hispanic whites will by the year 2050 make up 52 percent of the population in the United States, down from 74 percent today. Roughly 85 percent of recent immigrants come from Asia and Latin America and about 10 percent arrive from Europe. See Philip Martin and Elizabeth Midgley, "Immigration to the United States: Journey to an Uncertain Destination," *Population Bulletin* 49, 2 (1994): 5–9.

2. Bean et al., *Opening and Closing the Doors*, 1, 20–23. A more recent (1992) INS study estimated that 300,000 illegal immigrants settle in the United States each year. Cited in Martin and Midgley, "Immigration to the United States," 4. See also the subsequent discussion.

3. See Bean et al., *Opening and Closing the Doors*.

4. Katharine Donato, Jorge Durand, and Douglas Massey, in "Stemming the Tide? Assessing the Deterrent Effects of the Immigration Reform and Control Act," *Demography* 29, 2 (May 1992): 155, write that once "people begin migrating, they are very likely to make additional trips, and once a sufficient number of people have become involved in the process, social ties between U.S. employers, migrants and others form to facilitate the movement of new migrants and to encourage the repeated movement of experienced migrants."

5. The term comes from Peter H. Schuck, "The Transformation of Immigration Law," *Columbia Law Review* 84, 1 (1984): 1–90.

6. Ibid., 1–2.

7. House Committee on the Judiciary, *Grounds for Exclusion of Aliens under the Immigration and Nationality Act*, report prepared by Joyce Vialet, 100 Cong., 2d sess., 1988, Committee Print 7, 5 (hereafter referred to as Judiciary, *Grounds for Exclusion*).

8. These issues are discussed at great depth in James H. Kettner, *The Development of American Citizenship, 1608–1870* (Chapel Hill: University of North Carolina Press, 1978). See also discussion in Sophie Body-Gendrot and Martin A. Schain, "National and Local Politics and the Development of Immigration Policy," in Donald L. Horowitz and Gérard Noiriel, eds., *Immigrants in Two Democracies* (New York: New York University Press, 1992), 413–15.

9. Peter Schuck and Rogers M. Smith, *Citizenship without Consent* (New Haven: Yale University Press, 1985), 1–2.

10. Kettner, *The Development of American Citizenship*, 3–9, 74.

11. Ibid., 143–208, 231–40. Schuck and Smith, in *Citizenship without Consent*, 50–54, note that the ascriptive principle that birth determines citizenship has vied with consensual principles in defining membership in the American polity. The Constitution, they point out, requires that the president be a "natural-born Citizen," implying that citizenship would be acquired by birth. A number of reasons explain why, according to Schuck and Smith, Americans resisted a full-blown liberal consensualism. First, the newborn American states needed the support of all native-born residents in order to securely establish themselves and in order to seize

the property of supporters of the Crown. Second, birthright citizenship was viewed as an incentive to attract new families to settle there. Third, the courts feared in the nineteenth century that rejecting birthright citizenship would imply an unlimited right to expatriation. Finally, the courts did not want to delve too deeply into the issue of the basis of citizenship in order not to exacerbate sectional rivalries or conflicts about state-federal relations.

12. Yehoshua Arieli, *Individualism and Nationalism in American Ideology* (Cambridge, Mass.: Harvard University Press, 1964).

13. Some regulation was undertaken by states with large ports of entry. Between 1820 and 1860 these states passed laws to reduce costs associated with immigration regulation. For example, New York developed a reporting system to identify the infirm and destitute who might become wards of the state and who then instead could be deported. See William Bernard, "Immigration: History of U.S. Policy," in Stephan Thernstrom, ed., *Harvard Encyclopedia of American Ethnic Groups* (Cambridge, Mass.: Belknap Press, 1980), 488.

14. Schuck, "The Transformation of Immigration Law," 9.

15. Rogers Smith has recently challenged the Tocquevillean thesis. He notes the inegalitarian institutions of ascriptive hierarchy that have applied to racial and ethnic minorities and women through most of American history. Although his observation is valid, he loses sight, it would appear, of a larger point. American political founding principles *were* universal while, at the same time, those principles were in tension with prevailing practices. The fact of the matter is that excluded groups, such as blacks and women, could use those same principles to be later included in the body politic. If the principles were particularistic, a new nation made of new cloth with different principles would have had to be established in order to be more inclusive. Particularistic principles are evident in, for example, German concepts of nationhood, where national identity is ethnically *fixed* in the bloodline of the *Volk*. No endogenous tension exists whereby other groups could possibly claim to be "German." See Smith, "Beyond Tocqueville, Myrdal and Hartz: The Multiple Traditions in America," *American Political Science Review* 87, 3 (1993): 549–66. As Tom Paine put it, in *Common Sense* (London: Penguin Books, 1976 [1776]), 85, "But admitting we were all of English descent, what does it amount to? Nothing."

16. Figure for 1980 cited in Jeffrey Passel and Karen Woodrow, *Immigration to the United States*, rev. ed. (Washington, D.C.: Bureau of the Census, 1989). Figure for 1910 from Department of Commerce, *Statistical Abstract of the United States* (Washington, D.C.: Government Printing Office, 1913).

17. Bernard, "Immigration," 489.

18. Ibid., 490, and Judiciary, *Grounds for Exclusion*, 5–16.

19. Robert A. Devine, *American Immigration Policy, 1924–1952* (New Haven: Yale University Press, 1957), 5.

20. In 1911 and 1912 the figures remained about 850,000 but rose to about 1.2 million in each of the two following years. Figures from Immigration and Naturalization Service, *Statistical Yearbook of the Immigration and Naturalization Service* (Washington, D.C.: Government Printing Office, various years) (hereafter referred to collectively as INS statistical yearbooks).

21. See Judiciary, *Grounds for Exclusion*, 5–24, and Devine, *American Immigration Policy*, 5–23, 26–51.

22. Devine, *American Immigration Policy*, 5–23, 26–51.

23. Ibid.

24. Judiciary, *Grounds for Exclusion*, 23–24.

25. INS statistical yearbooks.

26. See Divine, *American Immigration Policy*, 113–45.

27. S. Rept. 1515, 81st Cong., 2d sess. (1950), p. 455; cited in Congressional Research Service Report, *U.S. Immigration Law and Policy: 1952–1986* (Washington, D.C.: Government Printing Office, December 1987), 4 (hereafter referred to as CRS, *Immigration Law*).

28. Divine, *American Immigration Policy*, 161.

29. Samuel Huntington, *American Politics: The Promise of Disharmony* (Cambridge, Mass.: Harvard University Press, 1981).

30. Quoted in CRS, *Immigration Law*, 1–2.

31. Ibid., 11, 20–21, 47–48.

32. David M. Reimers discusses the unexpected outcomes of the 1965 legislation in *Still the Golden Door: The Third World Comes to America* (New York: Columbia University Press, 1985), 74–76, 94–100.

33. Ibid.

34. Ibid., 241.

35. Divine, *American Immigration Policy*, 50.

36. Reimers, *Still the Golden Door*, 39–41.

37. See CRS, *Immigration Law*, 25–35; CRS cites Eleanor Hadley, "A Critical Analysis of the Wetback Problem," *Law and Contemporary Problems* (Duke University School of Law) 21 (spring 1965): 336.

38. CRS, *Immigration Law*, 39–42.

39. INS statistical yearbooks; Reimers, *Still the Golden Door*, 200–205, and CRS, *Immigration Law*, 86.

40. Passel and Woodrow, *Immigration to the United States*, 5–9.

41. See Rita J. Simon, "Immigration and American Attitudes," *Public Opinion* 10 (July–August 1987): 47–50.

42. Passel and Woodrow, *Immigration to the United States*, 12–14. A more recent INS study put the illegal population in the United States in 1992 at about 3.4 million—a remarkable figure given the IRCA effort. The 1992 figure is cited in Martin and Midgley, "Immigration to the United States," 19. The INS began collecting the nationality of apprehended aliens in fiscal 1988. In 1992, almost 96 percent of those apprehended gave Mexico as their domicile. See Immigration and Naturalization Service, *1992 Statistical Yearbook of the Immigration and Naturalization Service* (Washington, D.C.: Government Printing Office, 1993), 153.

43. Thomas Espenshade, Frank Bean, Tracy Goodis, and Michael White, "Immigration Policy in the United States: Future Prospects for the Immigration Reform and Control Act of 1986," in Godfrey Roberts, ed., *Population Policy: Contemporary Issues* (New York: Praeger, 1990), 75–76.

44. See, for example, Wayne A. Cornelius and Philip L. Martin, "The Uncertain Connection: Free Trade and Rural Mexican Migration to the United States,"

International Migration Review 27, 3 (1993): 484–512. One estimate has NAFTA producing an additional 20,000 to 30,000 illegal immigrants from Mexico throughout the 1990s, but reducing illegal immigration well below present levels in the beginning of the next century. See Philip Martin, *Trade and Migration: NAFTA and Agriculture* (Washington, D.C.: Institute for International Economics, 1993); cited in Martin and Midgley, "Immigration to the United States," 20.

45. See, in the case of California, for example, Thomas Muller and Thomas Espenshade, *The Fourth Wave: California's Newest Immigrants* (Washington, D.C.: Urban Institute, 1985).

46. Bean et al., *Opening and Closing the Doors*, 21.

47. Harris N. Miller, "'The Right Thing To Do': A History of Simpson-Mazzoli," in Nathan Glazer, ed., *Clamor at the Gates* (San Francisco: ICS, 1985), 49–52.

48. See Simon, "Immigration and America Attitudes."

49. CRS, *Immigration Law*, 25.

50. Reimers, *Still the Golden Door*, 203.

51. Miller, "The Right Thing," 53–54, and CRS, *Immigration Law*, 86–90.

52. U.S. Select Commission on Immigration and Refugee Policy, *U.S. Immigration Policy and the National Interest* (Washington, D.C.: Government Printing Office, 1981): 1–45.

53. Lawrence H. Fuchs, "The Search for a Sound Immigration Policy: A Personal View," in Glazer, *Clamor at the Gates*, 21–22.

54. Select Commission, *Immigration Policy*, 45–85. See also, CRS, *Immigration Law*, 91.

55. Miller, "The Right Thing," 55.

56. *Washington Post*, April 28, 1981; cited in Reimers, *Still the Golden Door*, 154.

57. Miller, "The Right Thing," 57.

58. Ibid., 60–67, and CRS, *Immigration Law*, 93–100.

59. CRS, *Immigration Law*.

60. Ibid., 101–5.

61. Romano Mazzoli, "Immigration Reform: The Path to Passage and Beyond," *Journal of Legislation* 14, 1 (1987): 41.

62. Public Law 603, 99th Cong., 2d sess. (November 6, 1986), *Immigration Reform and Control Act of 1986.*

63. See Bean et al., *Opening and Closing the Doors*, 25–34.

64. Immigration and Naturalization Service, *1989 Statistical Yearbook of the Immigration and Naturalization Service* (Washington, D.C.: Government Printing Office, 1990), xxiv–xxv; INS, *1992 Statistical Yearbook*, 13, 18; and Bean et al., *Opening and Closing the Doors*, 39.

65. Bean et al., *Opening and Closing the Doors*, 48–50. Court challenges involved issues of interpretation by the INS, such as the denial of eligibility to undocumented aliens in the country prior to 1982 who had left for a short absence and reentered with a nonimmigrant visa; the use of past rather then future employment ability as the measure of likelihood of becoming a public charge; and the policy of deporting persons eligible for legalization because they are in exclusion proceedings.

66. Ibid., 40–54. See also Doris Meissner and D. G. Papademetriou, *The Legalization*

Countdown: A Third-Quarter Assessment (Washington, D.C.: Carnegie Endowment, 1988), and David North and Anna Mary Portz, *Through the Maze: An Interim Report on the Alien and Legalization Program* (Washington, D.C.: Transcentury Development Associates, 1988); both cited in Bean et al., *Opening and Closing the Doors*, 40.

67. Bean et al., *Opening and Closing the Doors*, 59.

68. Ibid., 82–84. Bean et al. cite Leo Chavez, "Settlers and Sojourners," *Human Organization* 47, 2 (1988): 95–107.

69. Bean et al., *Opening and Closing the Doors*, 82–90.

70. Consequently, they use a regression equation to separate out the contribution of IRCA to the number of linewatch apprehensions (apprehensions at the border itself, and not inside the country) since 1986. See Michael White, Frank Bean, and Thomas Espenshade, *The U.S. Immigration Reform and Control Act and Undocumented Migration to the United States* (Washington, D.C.: Urban Institute and the Rand Corporation, July 19, 1989), and INS, *1992 Statistical Yearbook*, 156. Where the figures reported differ between the INS yearbooks and the secondary source, I have used INS figures.

71. White et al., *U.S. Immigration Reform and Control Act,* also noted that the employer sanctions provision may lead to an additional drop in apprehensions as more employers become aware of the law against hiring unemployed workers. On the other hand, if enforcement of this provision proves ineffective, they wrote in 1989, the deterrent effect of IRCA will erode over time.

72. Ibid. The authors note that the model included variables that were expected to influence illegal border crossings and that this model displayed a very high degree of fit. This instills confidence in the belief that the results do indeed reflect illegal border crossings.

73. Katharine M. Donato, Jorge Durand, and Douglas S. Massey, "Stemming the Tide? Assessing the Deterrent Effects of the Immigration Reform and Control Act," *Demography* 29, 2 (May 1992): 139–57, and Thomas Espenshade, "Policy Influences on Undocumented Migration to the United States," *Proceedings of the American Philosophical Society* 136, 2 (1992): 188–207. See also Scott Armstrong, "Illegal Border Crossings Show Upward Trend," *Christian Science Monitor*, October 10, 1990, 1, and Richard Stevenson, "Growing Problem: Aliens with Fake Documents," *New York Times*, August 4, 1990, A1.

74. Other examples of (quasilegal) transnational relations are, if less visible, still evident: the City University of New York allows undocumented immigrants to attend any of its colleges if they can show that they have lived in New York State for at least one year and declare that they intend to permanently reside in the state. Mayor Dinkins of New York appealed to the U.N. missions to intercede with "their" respective constituencies in the city of New York in order to alleviate ethnic tensions. The municipal government in Boston ordered its police and social services to aid illegal aliens in the city, where many undocumented Irish aliens are resident. See the *New York Times*, August 4, 1989, B3, and June 19, 1990, B3.

75. Schuck, "The Transformation of Immigration Law," 42–57.

76. A three-year "transitional diversity program" reserved 40,000 visas for persons with U.S. job offers who come from thirty-six countries that were "adversely

affected" by the Immigration and Naturalization Act of 1965. Forty percent of the visas were reserved for Irish immigrants. Other countries that gained included Poland, Italy, Tunisia, and Egypt.

77. Public Law 649, 101st Cong., 2d sess. (November 29, 1990), *Immigration Act of 1990*, Sec. 301(a). About 55,000 visas were issued under the "family fairness" provision in 1992 with the same number allocated for 1993. See INS, *1992 Statistical Yearbook*, 13.

78. INS, *1992 Statistical Yearbook*, 131. Proposals to limit welfare benefits to citizens, however, sharply increased naturalization requests in 1995.

79. This is indicated in the median years of residence of permanent residents before naturalization: for Europeans the median was 7 years in 1965 and 11 years in 1992; for Asians 6 years in 1965 and 7 years in 1992; for North Americans 9 years in 1965 and 12 years in 1992; and for South Americans 7 years and 9 years respectively. The baseline here is 1965 since in that year ethnic preferences were dropped. See INS, *1992 Statistical Yearbook*, 126.

80. In *Immigrant America: A Portrait* (Berkeley: University of California Press, 1990), 94–142, Alejandro Portes and Rubén G. Rumbaut point out that three variables help explain in large part the national and regional differentiation of naturalization rates: geographical proximity (the further away the country of origin, the more likely is naturalization), educational levels (positively correlated), and the political origin of the migration. Thus geographic distance involves greater cost and effort in communication and travel to and from the "home" country, entrepreneurs or professionals are more likely to naturalize because they tend to be more heavily involved in issues than concern government (property regulations, for example), and groups like refugees or immigrants from Communist countries like China have an obvious interest in finalizing their status in the United States. See also Reed Ueda, *Postwar Immigrant America* (Boston: St. Martin's Press, 1994), 123.

81. Reed Ueda, "Naturalization and Citizenship," in Thernstrom, *Harvard Encyclopedia of American Ethnic Groups*, 748. With those qualifications, a 1936 study of a sample of immigrant males in New Haven, Connecticut, found that after fifteen years of residence naturalization rates were 61 percent for Italians, 76 percent for mostly Jewish Russians, and 79 percent for Germans. INS data show that 38.7 percent of the cohort of immigrants that arrived in 1977 had naturalized by the end of 1991: 27 percent of Europeans, 55 percent of Asians, and 28 percent of North Americans, among others. The latter study, however, is statistically of much greater reliability. See William S. Bernard, "Cultural Determinants of Naturalization," *American Sociological Review* 1 (December 1936): 946; and INS, *1992 Statistical Yearbook*, 152.

82. Fuchs, "The Search for a Sound Immigration Policy," 18.

83. See, for example, Julian Simon, *The Economic Consequences of Immigration* (New York: Basil Blackwell, 1990), and "More Immigration Can Cut the Deficit," *New York Times*, May 10, 1990, A17; Editorial, "Come One, Come All," *Barron's*, February 26, 1990, 9; and Editorial, "The Simpson Curtain," *Wall Street Journal*, February 1, 1990, A8. See also Ben Wattenberg and Karl Zinsmeister, "The Case for More Immigration," *Commentary*, April 1990, 19–25.

84. The media also seem subject to the principle that he who shouts loudest gets the most prominent billing. A top-billing, front-page story by Robert Suro in the *New York Times*, "1986 Amnesty Law Is Seen as Failing to Slow Alien Tide," on June 18, 1989, gave much space to critics' claims that IRCA was failing and claimed that the INS was "virtually alone" in asserting that sanctions had substantially cut down on illegal immigration. Two months later, on August 8, 1989, the Urban Institute-Rand Corporation study, which estimated IRCA was responsible for preventing the entry of some 700,000 illegal aliens from 1986 to 1988, was covered in a small article on page A16 of the New York paper.

85. Section 212(a)(28) of the Immigration and Nationality Act of 1952.

86. Judiciary, *Grounds for Exclusion*, 47–51.

87. D. Cooper, "Promised Land or Land of Broken Promises? Political Asylum in the United States," *Kentucky Law Journal* 76 (summer 1987–88): 932–47. On refugee admissions statistics, see Bean et al., *Opening and Closing the Doors*, 94.

88. Editorial, "Giving Sanctuary, Fairly," *New York Times*, July 24, 1990, A20.

89. See Public Law 101-649, Sec. 601(a).

90. See Public Law 101-649, and INS, *1992 Statistical Yearbook*, 13, A.2–2.

91. Johannes M. M. Chan, "The Right to Nationality as a Human Right," *Human Rights Law Journal* 12 (February 28, 1991): 1.

92. Tomas Hammar, "Citizenship: Membership of a Nation and of a State," *International Migration* 24 (1986): 735–47; William Rogers Brubaker, "Membership without Citizenship," in *Immigration and the Politics of Citizenship in Europe and North America* (Lanham, Md.: University Press of America, 1989), 145–62; and Yasemin Nuhoğlu Soysal, "Limits of Citizenship: Guest workers in the Contemporary Nation-State System" (Ph.D. diss., Stanford University, 1991), 201–19.

93. There are also substantive legal reasons for viewing the shifts in the basis of membership in terms of a recasting of nationality rather than using terms like *denizenship* or *postnational membership*. This will be discussed at greater length in the following chapter.

94. Martin Heisler, "Transnational Migration as a Small Window on the Diminished Autonomy of the Modern Democratic State," *Annals* (AAPSS) 485 (May 1986): 153–66.

95. Ibid. Quote from Michael Walzer, *Spheres of Justice: A Defense of Pluralism and Equality* (New York: Basic Books, 1983), 39.

96. Gary Freeman, "Migration and the Political Economy of the Welfare State," *Annals* (AAPSS) 485 (May 1986): 60–63.

97. Layton-Henry writes that all "residents normally have some legal and civil rights. . . . there is a continuum of rights attached to membership of a state rather than a sharp distinction between member and non-member, citizen and non-citizen." See "The Challenge of Political Rights," in Zig Layton-Henry, ed., *The Political Rights of Migrant Workers in Western Europe* (London: Sage, 1990), 18.

98. See Hammar, "Citizenship."

4   Western Europe and the Age of Rights

1. R. J. Vincent, *Human Rights and International Relations* (Cambridge: Cambridge University Press, 1986), 44.
2. Human rights is not the only area where transnational mechanisms have come into play. Transnational commercial litigation has also dramatically expanded in this same period. See Harold Hongju Koh, "Transnational Public Law Litigation," *Yale Law Journal* 100 (1991): 2365.
3. Martin Shapiro and Alec Stone, "The New Constitutional Politics of Europe," *Comparative Political Studies* 26, 4 (January 1994): 402, 404, 409.
4. See Vincent, *Human Rights and International Relations*, 44–47, and Louis B. Sohn, "The New International Law: Protection of the Rights of Individuals Rather than States," *American University Law Review* 32, 1, (fall 1982): 1–64.
5. Louis Henkin, *The Age of Rights* (New York: Columbia University Press, 1990), 1–5.
6. The exact role of international human rights codes vis-à-vis the state is debated. My interest concerns the degree to which individuals and NGOs can make claims on the state in terms of those codes. See Henkin, ibid., 34.
7. The phrase is from Vincent, *Human Rights and International Relations*, 128.
8. The Foreign Relations Law of the United States defines customary international law as that law which "results from a general and consistent practice of states [which is] followed by them from a sense of legal obligation." American Law Institute, *Restatement of the Law Third: The Foreign Relations Law of the United States* (St. Paul, Minn.: The Institute, 1987), sec. 102.
9. A state that has not ratified the American convention is not subject to the jurisdiction of the Inter-American Court of Human Rights. Thus, the United States does not have to answer to the Inter-American Court. In contrast, Council of Europe member states are subject to the jurisdiction of the European convention organs. This is a significant difference, as will become apparent in the subsequent discussion. The human rights regime of the Organization of American States Charter is, however, an instrument that can be drawn upon within the U.S. courts.
10. Jörg Polakiewicz and Valérie Jacob-Foltzer, "The European Human Rights Convention in Domestic Law," *Human Rights Law Journal* 12 (March 28, 1991): 65–66. Quote from European Commission Case of *Chrysostomos and Others v. Turkey*, March 4, 1991.
11. See F. G. Jacobs, *The European Convention on Human Rights* (Oxford: Clarendon Press, 1975), 276–80. On the Court of Justice's decisions, see Andrew Evans, "Nationality Law and European Integration," *European Law Review* 16, 3 (1991): 205. Although the treaty establishing the European Economic Community does not contain a bill of rights, the European Court of Justice has been very active in guarding against community legislation that may violate human rights as defined by the ECHR and the constitutional traditions of member states. See Joseph H. H. Weiler, "Eurocracy and Distrust: Some Questions concerning the Role of the European Court of Justice in the Protection of Fundamental Human Rights within the Legal Order of the European Communities," *Washington Law Review* 61 (July 1986): 1105.

12. Rosalyn Higgins, "The European Convention on Human Rights," in Theodor Meron, *Human Rights in International Law* (Oxford: Clarendon Press, 1984), 495.

13. That the capitalist West drew on international human rights in the conflict with communism would not have surprised the likes of Adam Smith (in the *Wealth of Nations*, 1776) and Immanuel Kant (in "Zum Ewigen Frieden," 1795) who saw "free trade," world peace, and human rights as indivisible. See discussion in Fritz Fabricus, *Human Rights and European Politics* (Oxford: Berg, 1992), 17–18.

14. A. H. Robertson, *Human Rights in Europe*, 2d ed. (Manchester: Manchester University Press, 1977), 1–10.

15. On the status of nonnationals and the ECHR, see East African Asians case, discussed later in this chapter.

16. See the discussion in J. G. Merrills, *The Development of International Law by the European Court of Human Rights* (Manchester: Manchester University Press, 1988), 187–204.

17. Higgins, "The European Convention on Human Rights," 495–98.

18. L. Mikaelson, *European Protection of Human Rights* (Germantown, Md.: Sithoff and Noordhoff, 1980), 157–58. See Commission rulings in 434/58:2 *Yearbook* 354, 372, and 238/56:1 *Yearbook* 205. (*Yearbook* here refers to the Council of Europe, *Yearbook on the European Convention of Human Rights* [The Hague: Martinus Nijhoff Publishers, various years]).

19. It must be stressed that transnational migrants contribute to a changing environment wherein international human rights become more salient. It is not a simple causal relationship. The international human rights instruments had to be available. Other factors are likely to have contributed to the new prominence of human rights as well. Once we have this changing environment, all kinds of parties can exploit the new circumstances, not only "migrants." Cases involving long-resident aliens, citizens with cross-border ties, citizens with domestic concerns not answered under national law, and others can all come to the fore in this new environment.

20. The machinery of the ECHR is described in the convention itself. The discussion here also draws from Thomas Buergenthal, *International Human Rights in a Nutshell* (St. Paul, Minn.: West, 1988), 81–122.

21. The court has ruled that it is competent in certain circumstances to review rulings of the commission concerning admissibility. See Merrills, *The Development of International Law by the European Court of Human Rights*, 44–47.

22. See Buergenthal, *International Human Rights*, 101–6.

23. Marc J. Bossuyt and Yolanda van den Bosch, "Judges and Judgments: 25 Years [of] Judicial Activity in the Court of Strasbourg," *Revue Belge de Droit International* 18, 2 (1984–85): 703–5.

24. Polakiewicz and Jacob-Foltzer, "The European Human Rights Convention in Domestic Law," 65–66, 75–81.

25. Ibid.

26. See Roger Kerridge, "The Incorporation of the European Convention on Human Rights into United Kingdom Domestic Law," in M. P. Furmston, R. Kerridge, and

B. E. Sufrin, eds., *The Effect on English Domestic Law of Membership of European Communities and of Ratification of the European Convention on Human Rights* (The Hague: Martinus Nijhoff, 1983), 247–82.

27. Shapiro and Stone, "The New Constitutional Politics," 415.

28. Jacobs, *The European Convention on Human Rights*, 272.

29. Bossuyt and Van den Bosch, "Judges and Judgments," 712.

30. See data in Council of Europe, *Stocktaking on the European Convention on Human Rights: The First Thirty Years* (Strasbourg: Council of Europe, 1984).

31. Bossayt and Van den Bosch, "Judges and Judgments," 705–6; and Buergenthal, *International Human Rights*, 108; European Court of Human Rights, *Survey of Activities* (Strasbourg: Council of Europe, 1959–91, 1992, and 1993).

32. Compiled from data in the reports of the Council of Europe, *Stocktaking on the European Convention on Human Rights*, for the years 1979, 1982, and 1984. In 1976, 23 percent of registered applications were lodged by alien applicants, 27 percent in 1977, 14 percent in 1979, 20 percent in 1980, 18 percent in 1981, 25 percent in 1982, and 26 percent in 1983. In registered applications concerning the Federal Republic of Germany 32 percent and 38 percent of applicants were aliens in 1976 and 1977 respectively.

33. The proportion of the foreign population in 1980 was 6.8 percent in France, 7.2 percent in Germany, 5.1 percent in Sweden, and 14.1 percent in Switzerland. By 1990 Germany's foreign population proportion was 8.2 percent, France's was 6.4 percent, and Sweden's was 5.6 percent. The figures in the mid-1970s were only slightly different from the 1980 figures. See OECD, *SOPEMI: Trends in International Migration*, (Paris: OECD, 1992), 131. The first figure for France dates from 1982. See discussion in Martin Baldwin-Edwards and Martin Schain, "The Politics of Immigration," *West European Politics* 17, 2 (1994): 1–16.

34. The Commission of Human Rights, in 434/58: 2 *Yearbook* 372.

35. Progress has been made in international law on directly recognizing a right to nationality as a human right, as well. See Johannes M. M. Chan, "The Right to a Nationality as a Human Right," *Human Rights Law Journal* 12 (February 28, 1991): 1–14.

36. Council of Europe, *Stocktaking on the European Convention on Human Rights*, 154–56; and Richard Plender, *International Migration Law* (Dordrecht: Martinus Nijhoff, 1988), 228.

37. See "Case of Abdulaziz, Cabales and Balkandali," in Vincent Berger, *Case Law of the European Court of Human Rights, 1960–1987* (Dublin: UNIFO Publishers, 1989), 293–96. See also Ralph Beddard, *Human Rights and Europe* (London: Sweet and Maxwell, 1980), 62–67.

38. Jacobs, *The European Convention on Human Rights*, 164–66, 184–87; Zain M. Nedjati, *Human Rights under the European Convention* (Amsterdam: North-Holland, 1978), 136–37; and J. E. S. Fawcett, *The Application of the European Convention on Human Rights* (Oxford: Clarendon Press, 1969), 58–65.

39. The EC, the precursor of the EU, was in fact three European communities that were merged together in 1967. The three communities consisted of the European

Coal and Steel Community (founded in 1952), the European Atomic Energy Community (1958), and the more familiar European Economic Community.

40. See Jan Niessen, "European Community Legislation and Intergovernmental Co-operation on Migration," *International Migration Review* 26, 2 (1992): 676–77.

41. It is illustrative of the economistic and positivistic bent of much of social science, including international relations, that the European Court of Human Rights has been largely ignored while the EU has, of course, been the focus of much attention. It is much easier, apparently, to focus on "hard phenomena" like state bureaucracies, economics, "actors," and the like than to draw out the implications of states as ontologically and legally "constituted" entities whose purposes, interests, and *raison* can change.

42. This discussion and the discussion that follows draw from Giuseppe Callovi, "Regulation of Immigration in 1993: Pieces of the European Community Jig-Saw Puzzle," *International Migration Review* 26, 2 (1993): 353–72.

43. Quoted in ibid., 358.

44. Ibid., 359–72.

45. Quoted in ibid., 362. The Schengen agreement took effect in March 1995.

46. Yasemin Nuhoğlu Soysal, "Immigration and the Emerging European Polity," in Svein S. Andersen and Kjell A. Eliassen, eds., *Making Policy in Europe* (London: Sage, 1993), 171–86. It is noteworthy that the EU's law, unlike the ECHR, has direct effect over all member states and prevails over domestic law. If a human rights issue arises under the Treaty of Rome, it can be referred to the European Court of Justice but proceedings first have to commence in a national court. The European Parliament does have a human rights subcommittee whose mandate is to consider human rights on a global level. Finally, since 1987 every EU citizen has had the right to submit written petitions to the Parliament on EU matters including related human rights matters. In 1988–89, 692 petitions were admitted, of which 212 concerned human rights matters. See Kevin Boyle, "Europe: The Council of Europe, the CSCE, and the European Community," in Hurst Hannum, ed., *Guide to International Human Rights Practice*, 2d ed. (Philadelphia: University of Pennsylvania Press, 1992), 155.

5 The United States and the Age of Rights

1. In a letter from Jefferson as secretary of state to the French minister, M. Genet, on June 5, 1793; quoted in Harold Hongju Koh, "Transnational Public Law Litigation," *Yale Law Journal* 100 (1991): 2352–53.

2. 175 U.S. 677, 700 (1990).

3. Louis Henkin, *The Age of Rights* (New York: Columbia University Press, 1990) 144.

4. See Hurst Hannum, *Materials on International Human Rights and U.S. Constitutional Law* (Charlottesville, Va.: Procedural Aspects of International Law Institute, 1985), 4, and T. Franck and M. Glennon, *Foreign Relations and National Security Law* (St. Paul, Minn.: West, 1987), 96–99.

5. Gordon Christenson, "Using Human Rights Law to Inform Due Process and Equal Protection Clauses," *Cincinnati Law Review* 52 (1983): 3–37.

6. 26 F. Cas. 832, 847 (1822). See also discussion in Jeffrey M. Blum and Ralph G. Steinhardt, "Federal Jurisdiction over International Human Rights Claims: The Alien Test Claims Act after *Filartiga v. Pena-Irala*," *Harvard International Law Journal* 22, 1 (1981): 62.

7. Ibid., 60–62.

8. W. Michael Reisman, "Sovereignty and Human Rights in Contemporary International Law," *American Journal of International Law* 84 (1990): 870.

9. Thomas Buergenthal, *International Human Rights in a Nutshell* (St. Paul, Minn.: West, 1988), 216–17.

10. Hannum, *Materials on International Human Rights*, 36–37. Discrimination against aliens violates international law insofar as the discrimination concerns an international protected right. Discrimination against aliens *qua* aliens is not internationally outlawed. Thus, aliens' lack of voting rights is, for example, acceptable in international law.

11. The term *human rights*, with its connotation of transnational rights, is referred to in 19 federal cases prior to the twentieth century, 34 times from 1900 to 1944, 191 cases from 1945 to 1969, 803 cases in the 1970s, over 2,000 times in the 1980s, and, at the present rate, will be cited in over 4,000 cases through the 1990s. The term *immigrant* is used here in a broad sense. Aliens in general can, and have, taken advantage of international human rights law in cases before federal courts (see, for example, subsequent discussion on *Filartiga v. Pena-Irala*). Figures have been compiled by the author from legal database searches.

12. Theodor Meron, *Human Rights and Humanitarian Norms as Customary Law* (Oxford: Clarendon Press, 1989), 121–22.

13. 505 F. Supp. 787 (1980), affirmed on other grounds in *Rodriguez-Fernandez v. Wilkinson*, 654 F. 2d 1382 (10th Cir. 1981). See also the discussion in Farooq Hassan, "The Doctrine of Incorporation," *Human Rights Quarterly* 5 (1983): 68–86.

14. 505 F. Supp. 795.

15. Ibid.

16. 505 F. Supp. 787, 798.

17. "The United States," the court noted dryly, ". . . preaches incessantly about the superiority of its system as a bulwark for human rights." Ibid.

18. See "Constructing the State Extra-Territorially: Jurisdictional Discourse, the National Interest and Transnational Norms," *Harvard Law Review* 103 (1990): 1273. The anonymous author focuses, however, on American constitutional law and transnational activities, and not on international law as such.

19. See Robert J. Martineau, Jr., "Interpreting the Constitution: The Use of International Human Rights Norms," *Human Rights Quarterly* 5 (1983): 104. See also Hassan, "The Doctrine of Incorporation," 68–86.

20. 630 F. 2d 876 (1980).

21. See Koh, "Transnational Public Litigation," 2366.

22. See discussion in Blum and Steinhardt, "Federal Jurisdiction over International Human Rights Claims," 53–113.

23. "In light of," the court stated, ". . . the renunciation of torture . . . by virtually all

of the nations of the world (*in principle if not in practice*) we find that an act of torture . . . violates established norms of the international law of human rights . . ." (emphasis added). 630 F. 2d 876, 880.

24. 630 F. 2d 876, 877. See also Meron, *Human Rights and Humanitarian Norms*, 123–24.

25. David Bodansky, "Human Rights and Universal Jurisdiction," in Mark Gibney, ed., *World Justice? U.S. Courts and International Human Rights* (Boulder, Colo.: Westview Press), 1–22. Bodansky notes that if, for example, an American court prosecuted a Frenchman for smoking in the Louvre because it violated U.S. law prohibiting smoking in public places, France would have cause for complaint under international law. Legally, the concept of "universal jurisdiction" is not in question; which human rights violations are subject to universal jurisdiction is debated.

26. See, for example, Karen E. Holt, "*Filartiga v. Pena-Irala* after Ten Years: Major Breakthrough or Legal Oddity?" *Georgia Journal of International and Comparative Law* 20, 3 (1990): 543–69.

27. 457 U.S. 202 (1982).

28. 501 F. Supp., 544 (1980), affirmed sub. nom. *Plyler v. Doe*, 457 U.S. 202.

29. Meron, *Human Rights and Humanitarian Norms*, 124–25. See also Peter Schuck, "The Transformation of Immigration Law," *Columbia Law Review* 84, 1 (1984): 54–59, and R. B. Lillich, "The Role of Domestic Courts in Enforcing International Human Rights Law," in Hurst Hannum, ed., *Guide to International Human Rights Practice* (Philadelphia: University of Pennsylvania Press, 1984), 230–31. "To the extent," the court noted, "that the United States is neglecting its pledge to promote human rights or to exert the greatest efforts to further educational opportunities [of an alien], an alien's government may call the United States to answer before an international tribunal." 501 F. Supp., 544, 596.

30. Christenson, "Using Human Rights Law," 7.

31. Henkin, *The Age of Rights*, 128–29.

32. Ibid., 133, citing *Reid v. Covert* 354 U.S. at 5 (1957). On the reluctance of the Senate to ratify international human rights instruments, see also Henkin, "International Human Rights and Rights in the U.S.," in Theodor Meron, ed., *Human Rights in International Law* (Oxford: Clarendon Press, 1984), 50–55.

33. It has been argued that what was critical in the progress of international human rights law in domestic legal forums in Western Europe, compared with the slow progress in the United States, was that human rights law benefited from the institutional pressures involved in the project of European unity and "harmonization" policies. While there is merit to this argument, it overlooks the variations *between European countries* in adopting or acceding to international human rights law (for example, Article 25 of the European Convention on Human Rights). See Kathryn Sikkink, "The Political Power of Foreign Policy Ideas: The Origins of Human Rights Policy in the U.S. and Western Europe" (paper presented at the American Political Science Association, Washington, D.C., August 29–31, 1991).

34. Schuck, "The Transformation of Immigration Law," 57.

35. Memorial of the Government of the United States, Case Concerning U.S. Diplomatic and Consular Staff in Tehran (*U.S. v. Iran*) (International Court of Justice, January 1980), 71.
36. Kathryn Burke, Sandra Coliver, Connie de la Vega, and Stephen Rosenbaum, "Application of International Human Rights Law in State and Federal Courts," *Texas International Law Journal* 18 (1983): 321.
37. See CA Prop. 187 (1994).
38. See David Andrew Price, "But Who Should Pay?" *Washington Post*, November 13, 1994, C7; Robert Suro, "Two California Judges Block Anti-Immigrant Measures at the Start," *Washington Post*, November 10, 1994, A39; and Maura Dolan, "Parts of Prop. 187 May Be Blocked 2 or More Years," *Los Angeles Times*, November 16, 1994, A1.
39. The poll results respectively were conducted by Yankelovich Partners Inc. for Time and CNN, with 800 respondents, and by Princeton Survey Research Associates for Times Mirror, with a sample of 1,511. Both were conducted in early December 1994.
40. Martin Shapiro and Alec Stone, "The New Constitutional Politics of Europe," *Comparative Political Studies* 26, 4 (1994): 404, 409–11.
41. Koh notes how in the past two decades there has been a consistent decline in judicial deference to the notion of sovereignty. See Koh, "Transnational Public Law," 2392–93.

6 States without Nations

1. Noah Pickus, "Trans-national America? Separating Rights from Belonging" (presentation at Law and Society Annual Meeting, Phoenix, June 1994); Tomas Hammar, *Democracy and the Nation State* (Aldershot: Avebury, 1990); and Gidon Gottlieb, *Nation against State* (New York: Council of Foreign Relations, 1993).
2. Thus the flowering of nationalism in Eastern Europe and the former Soviet Union met with a West seeking out new political and social forms. "Paradoxically," Gottlieb writes, in *Nation against State*, p. 1, "the struggle for the creation of new states is taking place at a time when older states are moving toward broader associations and when the very notion of statehood has lost substance."
3. The OSCE is the node, to put it in more legal terms, in an "institutional dialogue" among "a diverse blend of institutions and regimes, regional and bipolar compacts, and national governmental actors," each with their own specific functions. Adapted from Harold Hongju Koh, "Transnational Public Law Litigation," *Yale Law Journal* 100 (1991): 2371, 2400, 2402.
4. For fifteen years, the OSCE had no formal organization. Instead, a series of follow-up conferences was instituted to provide a forum to review compliance by the participating states with their OSCE commitments. This forum also allowed for the OSCE codes to be amplified, amended, or reinterpreted. The Helsinki Final Act had four major chapters, or "baskets." Basket I dealt with various "Confidence-Building Measures." Basket II concerned cooperation in the areas of economics, science, technology, and the environment, and human rights were spelled out in Basket III. Basket IV outlined the process for the follow-up confer-

ences. The Paris meeting created a permanent structure for the OSCE. A permanent secretariat was found, to be seated in Prague, and a Conflict Prevention Centre (in Vienna) and an Office of Free Elections (in Warsaw) were created. Consultations, it was decided, would regularly take place on head of state, foreign minister, and senior official level. The charter also broke down the first three baskets into seven sections: the human dimension, security, economic cooperation, the environment, culture, immigrant workers, and the Mediterranean. See Thomas Buergenthal, "The CSCE and the Promotion of Racial and Religious Tolerance" (paper given at the International Legal Colloquium on Racial and Religious Hatred and Group Libel, Tel Aviv University, Tel Aviv, December 1991).

5. The OSCE is not a treaty or an international agreement that is legally binding on the signatories. Rather, the OSCE politically commits the participating states to a constitutional order as defined by the OSCE.

6. Suzanne Bastid, "The Special Significance of the Helsinki Final Act," in T. Buergenthal, ed., *Human Rights, International Law and the Helsinki Accord* (New York: Universe Books, 1977), 11–19.

7. CSCE: Charter of Paris for a New Europe, 30 *International Legal Materials* [I.L.M.] (1991), 190–208 (hereafter cited as Paris).

8. Ibid.

9. James Baker III, "CSCE in Copenhagen," *World Affairs* 153, 1, (summer 1990): 3.

10. Prague Meeting of the CSCE, 31 I.L.M. (1992), 979 (hereafter cited as Prague).

11. Copenhagen Meeting of the CSCE, 29 I.L.M. (1990), 1309 (hereafter cited as Copenhagen).

12. Ibid., 1311–15. See also Moscow Meeting of the CSCE, 30 I.L.M. (1991), 1681 (hereafter cited as Moscow).

13. Copenhagen, 1307–21.

14. See, for example, CSCE Council from the CSCE Seminar of Experts in Oslo, 31 I.L.M. (1992), 377 (hereafter cited as Oslo).

15. See Prague, 981, 986, 994.

16. Moscow, 1690–91.

17. See Copenhagen, 1309. States may develop their own political, social, economic, and cultural systems but only insofar as they conform with international law (thus constricting the state's room for maneuver considerably); see Copenhagen, 1308.

18. German unification, consequently, was not viewed as a threat but as a way of extending the human rights regime. See Paris, 198.

19. Oslo, 377.

20. See Moscow, 1688–90.

21. See Copenhagen, 1319, art. 38.

22. CSCE Meeting of Experts on National Minorities, 30 I.L.M. (1991), 1696 (hereafter cited as National Minorities).

23. National Minorities, 1695–96.

24. Copenhagen, 1319.

25. See Steven Erlanger, "Latvia Amends Harsh Citizenship Law That Angered Russia," *New York Times*, July 24, 1994, 3.

26. National Minorities, 1697, 1700–1702.

27. Ibid., 1698–99.

28. Ibid.
29. Ibid., 1697–98, 1700. See Copenhagen, 1318.
30. See, for example, Copenhagen, 1315.
31. National Minorities, 1696–97.
32. Thomas M. Franck, "The Emerging Right to Democratic Governance," *American Journal of International Law*, 86, 46 (1992): 50.
33. The sections that follow draw extensively from David Jacobson, "Conclusion: The Global Future," in David Jacobson, ed., *Old Nations, New World: Conceptions of World Order* (Boulder, Colo.: Westview Press, 1994): 218–24.
34. Additional criteria come into play in regional organizations like the EU. See Andrew Evans, "Nationality Law and European Integration," *European Law Review* 16, 3 (June 1991): 190–215.
35. Such universal criteria were detailed in the U.N. Protocol on Refugees and incorporated into domestic laws of many countries.
36. See Copenhagen, 1318, art. 32.4.
37. The concept of "weak" and "strong" ties to a state, in a transnational world, is discussed in "Constructing the State Extra-Territorially: Jurisdictional Discourse, the National Interest and Transnational Norms," *Harvard Law Review* 103 (1990): 1273.
38. Transnational activities are not necessarily bound by the boundaries of the Euro-Atlantic community. Japan, for example, is not a member of that community.
39. See "Constructing the State Extra-Territorially," 1284.
40. Theodor Meron, *Human Rights and Humanitarian Norms as Customary Law* (Oxford: Clarendon Press, 1989), 164–66. See also earlier discussion on the OSCE. Koh notes that "transnational public law" is unique in that it blends domestic litigation, in which claims are made between private individuals in domestic forums, and international litigation, in which states make claims upon one another based on treaty and international law before international tribunals. In transnational public law litigation, individuals, government officials, and states sue one another in a variety of forums, including national courts. "A broader look at the shape of international legal process reveals," writes Koh, "that we stand at a moment of startling, perhaps unprecedented, revival in transnational adjudication." See Koh, "Transnational Public Law," 2348, 2400. This parallels the growth of constitutional politics in Western Europe described by Martin Shapiro and Alec Stone, "The New Constitutional Politics of Europe," *Comparative Political Studies* 26, 4 (1994): 397–420.
41. Thus, for example, in being able to make claims on the courts in terms of international human rights codes, nonstate associations reproduce and realize those codes as the modality, the structure, of international order. That order exists only in virtue of being reproduced in this manner. Conversely, nonstate associations can only make such claims by presupposing the prior existence of an international order that recognizes such claims. The state, as the mediator and regulative mechanism, thus plays a critical role in facilitating and supporting a certain complex of "enduring relationships." See Roy Bhasker, *The Possibility of Naturalism* (Brighton: Harvester Press, 1979), 31–48, on "agency" and "struc-

ture." See also Pierre Bourdieu, *Outline of a Theory of Practice* (Cambridge: Cambridge University Press, 1977), 78.

42. In this way, the new international order breaks down the two-tiered structure of the system of states, where NGOs and citizens have agency within the state, and the state has agency in the international arena, into a single tier, where NGOs and individuals are the agents of a broader transnational community.

43. Koh, in "Transnational Public Law," 2349, 2371, characterizes the legal basis of the transnational order thus: "(1) a *transnational party structure*, in which states and nonstate entities equally participate; (2) a *transnational claim structure*, in which violations of domestic and international, private and public law are alleged in a single action; (3) a *prospective basis*, fixed as much upon obtaining judicial declaration of transnational norms as upon resolving past disputes; (4) . . . the *transportability of those norms* to other domestic and international fora . . .; and (5) a subsequent process of *institutional dialogue* among various domestic, international, judicial and political fora . . ." (emphasis in original).

44. "Constructing the State Extra-Territorially," 1297.

45. See Laurie Goodstein, "The Culture War Goes Global: The Latest Battlefield Is the Cairo Population Conference," *Washington Post*, September 4, 1994, C2.

46. U.N. Economic and Social Council, Forty-Eighth Session, *Procedure for Dealing with Communications Relating to Violations of Human Rights*, E/RES/1503 (XLVIII), June 19, 1970.

47. See "U.S. Human Rights Office Grows in Influence," *New York Times*, January 19, 1992, A5. See also T. Burgenthal, *International Human Rights in a Nutshell* (St. Paul, Minn.: West, 1988), 211–42, for discussion and bibliography on the topic. On the European case, see P. Sands, "Current Developments: E.C. Law [and] External Relations," *International and Comparative Law Quarterly*, 40, 3 (July 1991), 730–34.

48. See John S. Gibson, *International Organizations, Constitutional Law and Human Rights* (New York: Praeger, 1991), 168. Gibson cites Department of State, *Country Reports on Human Rights Practices for 1990* (Washington, D.C.: Department of State, 1991).

49. Meron, *Human Rights and Humanitarian Norms*, 208.

50. On the (former) Yugoslavia crisis, see Morton H. Halperin and David J. Scheffer, *Self-Determination in the New World Order* (Washington, D.C.: Carnegie Endowment for Peace, 1992), 32–44.

51. On the Chechen crisis and Euro-Atlantic responses see, for example, European Commission, "Declaration by the European Union on Chechnya," 1825th Council Meeting, Brussels, Press Release: PESC 007, January 23, 1995; "Council of Europe Looks to Expand," *Agence Europe*, February 1, 1995; Michael Binyon and Richard Beeston, "Russia: OSCE Ministers to Hold Emergency Talks on [Chechnya]," *Times* (London), January 5, 1995, 1; Tyler Marshall, "EU Delays Russia Pact over Chechnya," *Los Angeles Times*, January 6, 1995, 10; and "OSCE Willing to Cooperate towards Solution of Chechnya Conflict," *Agence Europe*, January 7, 1995.

52. See Moscow, 1677, art. 17.2.

53. Emanuel Adler, "Europe's New Security Order: A Pluralistic Security Commu-

nity," in Beverly Crawford, ed., *The Future of European Security* (Berkeley: International and Area Studies, University of California, 1992), 287-327.

54. Ibid. As Adler notes, "security communities" are also not to be confused with international regimes. International regimes are areas where expectations between states converge and are instituted in international arrangements (like GATT). Unlike in collective security arrangements, however, the sovereign state is still the organizing principle.

55. William Pfaff, "Baker's Commonwealth of Democracies," *International Herald Tribune*, June 26, 1991, 13, and "Baker Outlines Goal of Collective Peace," *International Herald Tribune*, April 22, 1992, 2. See also William Safire, "Right to Intervene," *New York Times*, November 30, 1992, A15.

56. Paris, 198.

57. See, for example, Samuel Kim, "Chinese Perspectives on World Order," in David Jacobson, ed., *Old Nations, New World: Conceptions of World Order* (Boulder, Colo.: Westview Press, 1994), 37-74.

58. Paris, 204.

7 Nations without States: Reflections on a Changing Landscape

1. As one suburban resident in San Diego put it, "It's like we're living in the Third World here. It doesn't seem to me this is part of the American Dream." See Roger Rouse, "Mexican Migration and the Social Space of Postmodernism," *Diaspora* 1, 1 (1991): 8-23; Rouse cites for the quotation Eric Bailey and H. G. Reza, "Illegals, Homeless Clash in S.D. County," *Los Angeles Times*, June 5, 1988, 1. See also discussion in Jack Citrin, Beth Reingold, and Donald P. Green, "American Identity and the Politics of Ethnic Change," *Journal of Politics* 52, 4 (1990): 1124-49. On the changing composition of foreigners in Europe, see Department of Economic and Social Development, *Report on the World Social Situation* (New York: United Nations, 1993), 18-19; and in the United States, see Philip Martin and Elizabeth Midgley, "Immigration to the United States: Journey to an Uncertain Destination," *Population Bulletin* 49, 2 (1994): 5-9.

2. As Arjun Appadurai notes, "Where soil and place were once the key to the linkage of territorial affiliation . . . key identities and identifications now only partially revolve around the realities and images of space." He adds that in the emerging postnational world, "diaspora runs with, not against, the grain of identity, movement and reproduction." See Appadurai, "The Heart of Whiteness," *Callaloo* 16, 4 (1993): 798, 803.

3. Among the growing literature on what is viewed as the decline of civil society and politics, see, inter alia, Robert Bellah, Richard Madsen, William M. Sullivan, Ann Swidler, and Steven M. Tipton, *Habits of the Heart* (Berkeley: University of California Press, 1985), and Richard Sennet, *The Fall of Public Man* (New York: Vintage Press, 1978).

4. See discussion in, inter alia, Morton H. Halperin and David J. Scheffer, *Self-Determination in the New World Order* (Washington, D.C.: Carnegie Endowment for Peace, 1992), 45-52.

5. See Benedict Anderson, *Imagined Communities: Reflections on the Origins and Spread of Nationalism* (London: Verso, 1983), 22-26.

6. Ibid., 18–20.
7. David Martin, *A General Theory of Secularization* (Oxford: Basil Blackwell, 1978), 4.
8. See also the discussion on religion and nationhood in George M. Thomas, *Revivalism and Cultural Change: Christianity, Nation Building and the Market in Nineteenth-Century United States* (Chicago: University of Chicago Press, 1989).
9. This paragraph draws from my discussion in "Introduction: The Global Present," in David Jacobson, ed., *Old Nations, New World: Conceptions of World Order* (Boulder, Colo.: Westview Press, 1994), 5.
10. See David Jacobson, "Protestantism, Authoritarianism, and Democracy: A Comparison of the Netherlands, the United States and South Africa," *Religion* 17 (July 1987): 275–301.
11. See Buckart Holzner and Roland Robertson, "Identity and Authority: A Problem Analysis of Processes of Identification and Authorization," in Holzner and Robertson, eds., *Identity and Authority* (New York: St. Martin's Press, 1979), 3–4.
12. See Michael Walzer, *The Revolution of the Saints* (Cambridge, Mass.: Harvard University Press, 1965).
13. H. Richard Niebuhr, "The Protestant Movement and Democracy in the United States," in J. W. Smith and A. L. Jamison, eds., *The Shaping of American Religion* (Princeton: Princeton University Press, 1961), 22–23.
14. See Jacobson, "Protestantism, Authoritarianism and Democracy," and Daniel Boorstin, *The Discoverers* (New York: Vintage Books, 1983), 566.
15. Quoted by André Du Toit from the *Zuid Afrikaan*, October 13, 1885, in his "'Puritans in Africa?' Afrikaner 'Calvinism' and Kupyerian Neo-Calvinism in Late Nineteenth South Africa," *Comparative Studies in Society and History* 27, 2 (1985): 233.
16. Donald W. Hanson, *From Kingdom to Commonwealth* (Cambridge, Mass.: Harvard University Press, 1970), 15–20, 340–43, and Walzer, *The Revolution of the Saints*, 4–10; Walzer cites Daniel Lerner, *The Passing of Traditional Society* (New York: Free Press of Glencoe, 1958). See also Marc Bloch, *Feudal Society*, trans. L. A. Manyon (Chicago: University of Chicago Press, 1961).
17. See Gianfranco Poggi, *The Development of the Modern State* (Stanford: Stanford University Press, 1978). See also the discussion in chap. 2.
18. *Richard II*, act 2, scene 1 (emphasis added), cited in A. W. Orridge, "Varieties of Nationalism," in Leonard Tivey, ed., *The Nation-State: The Formation of Modern Politics* (New York: St. Martin's, 1981), 40.
19. Cornelia Navari, "Origins of the Nation State," in Tivey, *The Nation-State: The Formation of Modern Politics*, 35.
20. Soldiers in their deaths mythically *embody* their country as expressed in the perhaps most remembered poetic lines about war, from Rupert Brooke's *The Soldier*:

> If I should die, think only this of me:
> That there's some corner of a foreign field
> That is for ever England.

Soldiers' deaths signify, paradoxically, the immortal quality of the nation itself—through war memorials, remembrances, and cemeteries.

21. Mircea Eliade, *The Sacred and the Profane: The Nature of Religion* (New York: Harcourt, Brace and World, 1957), 20–65.

22. Eliade himself assumes incorrectly that the modern state is a "profane" entity. See ibid.

23. This is why the numerous studies, particularly in the United States, on the economic benefits or costs of illegal immigrants miss the point—or at least the principle issue.

24. Joseph R. Strayer and Dana Munro, *The Middle Ages* (New York: Appleton-Century-Crofts, 1959), 115, and Perry Anderson, *Lineages of the Absolutist State* (London: New Left Books, 1974), 37–38; both cited and quoted in John Gerard Ruggie, "Territoriality and Beyond: Problematizing Modernity in International Relations," *International Organization* 47, 1 (1993): 149–50.

25. Eliade, *The Sacred and the Profane*, 23–24.

26. See Anderson, *Imagined Communities*, 15–16.

27. Eliade, *The Sacred and the Profane*, 57.

28. Jürgen Habermas, "Citizenship and National Identity," *Praxis International* 12, 1 (1992): 7.

29. A growing literature calls for creating international legal guarantees for minority rights within the nation-state framework (see discussions in, for example, Halperin and Scheffer, *Self-Determination in the New World Order*; Anthony Anghie, "Human Rights and Cultural Identity: New Hope for Ethnic Peace?" *Harvard International Law Journal* 33, 2 (1992): 341–52; R. Cholewinski, "The Racial Discrimination Convention and the Protection of Cultural and Linguistic Ethnic Minorities," *Revue de Droit International* 69, 3 (1991): 157–253; Hurst Hannum, *Autonomy, Sovereignty, and Self-Determination: The Accommodation of Conflicting Rights* (Philadelphia: University of Pennsylvania Press, 1990); and Hurst Hannum, "Contemporary Developments in the International Protection of the Rights of Minorities," *Notre Dame Law Review* 66 (1991), 1431–48. There are a number of problems with this approach. It tends to view that international human rights law is subsidiary to interstate law (which, of course, describes the traditional paradigm); if accurate, such an approach is likely to fail vis-à-vis state assertions of sovereignty and national self-determination. Indeed, such an approach failed on just such grounds when minority rights were propagated under the League of Nations (see Stephan Ryan, *Ethnic Conflict and International Relations* [Hants: Dartmouth Publishing, 1990], 155–60). More important, such an approach does not recognize, as proposed here, the emerging importance of NGOs (including ethnic associations) as international actors in their own right.

30. Richard K. Betts, "Systems of Peace or Causes of War? Collective Security, Arms Control and the New Europe," *International Security* 17, 1 (1992): 5–43. See also discussion in Malcom Chalmers, "Beyond the Alliance System," *World Policy Journal* 7, 2 (1990): 215–50; and Gregory Flynn and David J. Scheffer, "Limited Collective Security," *Foreign Policy* 80 (fall 1990): 77–101.

31. See Moscow Meeting of the CSCE, 30 I.L.M. (1991), p. 1677, art. 17.2, linking

collective action to support "legitimate" governments—that is, democratically elected governments dedicated to human rights—in threat of being overthrown.

32. Halperin and Scheffer describe how human rights have come to define the politics of recognition and intervention in their *Self-Determination in the New World Order*. On the other hand, the crisis in the former Yugoslavia also demonstrates the poverty of imagination and the inertia of institutions, as a colleague of mine has pointed out, in the Vance-Owen plan, which reverts to (as it turns out, futile) territorial "solutions."

33. The consociational model, with its segmental institutional pattern, may become more prevalent. See David Jacobson, "How Far Can the United States Stretch Its Borders?" *Haaretz*, November 27, 1991, B1 (in Hebrew).

34. Anderson in his *Imagined Communities* describes how important print capitalism was in making it possible for large numbers of people to relate themselves to others such that imagined communities could, indeed, be imagined. Similarly, satellite television is creating all kinds of new possibilities; for example, ethnic programs can now be broadcast internationally. The possibility exists for a Turk in Germany to watch the local news from Istanbul—a graphic illustration of the translocalization of the neighborhood referred to earlier.

Index